THE
HUMAN
FACTOR
IN COMPUTER
CRIME

J. Van Duyn

PETROCELLI BOOKS
Princeton, New Jersey

Copyright © 1985 Petrocelli Books, Inc.
All rights reserved.

Designed by Diane L. Backes
Typesetting by Backes Graphics

Printed in the United States of America
First printing

Library of Congress Cataloging in Publication Data

Van Duyn, J.A., 1926–
   The human factor in computer crime.

   Bibliography: p.
   Includes index.
   1. Computer crimes—United States. 2. Electronic
data processing departments—Security measures.
I. Title.
HV6773.2.V36   1984   364.1'68   84-20620
ISBN 0-89433-256-2

Contents

ONE   **Introduction**   **1**

    1.1 The Foreign Corrupt Practices Act
        of 1977
    1.2 The Privacy Act of 1974
    1.3 The Export Administration Act of 1979
    1.4 The California Penal Code
    1.5 States Computer Crime Laws
    1.6 Federal Computer Crime Bill

TWO   **Establishing Computer Security**   **17**

    2.1 Management Security Philosophy
    2.2 Difference in Security Approaches
        to Centralized and Distributed Data
        Processing
    2.3 Risk Analysis
    2.4 Risk Management
    2.5 Security Policy and Standards Manuals
    2.6 Updating Procedures

THREE **Physical Security**   **33**

    3.1 Building and Parking Lot Security
    3.2 Physical Access Control
    3.3 Fire Security/Protection

3.4 Housekeeping in Computer and Storage Rooms

3.5 Air Conditioning System

FOUR   **Hardware Security**   **45**

4.1 Electric Power

4.2 Terminals

4.3 Data Communications/Network Lines

FIVE   **Software Security**   **59**

5.1 The EDP Auditor's Role

5.2 Systems Controls

5.3 Applications Controls

5.4 DP Crime Methods, Detection and Countermeasures, and Potential Perpetrators

SIX   **Personnel Security**   **93**

6.1 Background Investigation

6.2 Career-Pathing

6.3 Possible Indicators of Discontentment

6.4 Proper Security Orientation for New DP Employees

6.5 Separation of Duties of DP Staff

6.6 Effective Performance Evaluation Systems

6.7 Rotating Personnel Duties

6.8 The Budget Control Issue in DP Security

6.9 Cognitive Style Positioning

SEVEN   **Contingency and Disaster Recovery Planning   129**

7.1 A Contingency Plan

7.2 A Disaster Recovery Plan

7.3 Side Effects

7.4 Solutions to Avoid Any Such Possible Problems

EIGHT **EDP Insurance**   143

    8.1 EDP Insurance versus General Insurance
    8.2 Vulnerable Areas and Risks
    8.3 Areas Covered by EDP Insurance
    8.4 White-Collar Computer Crime Insurance
    8.5 Individual Bonding

Glossary   151

Bibliography   157

Index   161

ACKNOWLEDGEMENTS

Among the many people who have helped shape this book and to whom I'm most grateful, I want to convey a special thanks to Dr. Ned Chapin for his incisive review and constructive suggestions. In addition, I wish to express my appreciation to the following individuals for their valuable help and cooperation:

Dean B. Allison Assistant United States
Attorney Chief, Major Frauds Unit
Los Angeles, California

Joe A. Nunez
Assistant Supervisor
Records & Exhibit Section
Los Angeles, California

Robert E. Killion, CSR
Official Court Reporter
Los Angeles, California

J. Van Duyn

1

Introduction

ONE
Introduction

To appreciate the extent to which human factor plays a part in computer crime, we have to be aware of its role in crime deterrence, prevention, detection, and risk assessment on the physical, hardware, software, and personnel security levels.

Considering the rather recent appreciation of the last security category, perhaps it isn't odd that at most DP facilities while great attention is afforded to physical, hardware, and software security measures and controls, little or no thought is given to personnel security. Yet, without effective personnel security, meaning a security program which is designed to foster the most effective deterrent against computer crime: *job satisfaction,* the most sophisticated hardware and software security systems are worthless.

This does not mean to imply that the first three computer security categories are not important insofar as computer crime countermeasures are concerned. Far from it.

Nevertheless, unless the human factor—an element often ignored by management and neglected by high technology technicians—is considered in every aspect of computer security, the business or government organization and its DP operations are highly vulnerable to computer crime, as the case histories offered in this book indicate.

The examples presented here also help to separate the myth and the recent nationwide hype about outsiders being the greatest threat to business and government DP security. The truth is that insiders pose a far greater threat to the organization's computer security than outside "electronic invaders" possibly could. The reason is pure and simple. Insiders are familiar with their employer's DP operations and the type of data each system and application is storing and processing. Consequently, they know where to look for specific data. And if they are in doubt, they can reference the systems' documentation which usually includes programming specifications, file and record layouts, a data element dictionary, and so on. But most significantly, insiders have or can somehow get the password to access stored crucial information such as financial, marketing, manufacturing, technological, or research data *unless* proper prevention and detection measures are in effect.

Before going any further, perhaps a definition of computer security is appropriate. Computer security, according to computer crime experts, is an umbrella that protects the organization's hardware and software, as well as the data and information processed by the computer against abuse, fraud, embezzlement, sabotage, and intentional or accidental damage, or natural disaster.

And who has the awesome responsibility to ensure that effective measures are installed and maintained? In the final analysis the security of the organization's computer equipment—the raw and processed data and information, *and* the personnel using these valuable resources—is the responsibility of top management.

4

Moreover, because computer security is a *management issue,* management must define and enunciate its *security philosophy* BEFORE setting up a computer security system, and perhaps even BEFORE a risk assessment is performed.

In balancing risk assessment with the level of risk the company can accept and the cost of computer security, the following legislative and regulatory requirements should be considered by management:

1.1 THE FOREIGN CORRUPT PRACTICES ACT OF 1977

Because by now all accounting and record keeping functions in both commercial and government organizations are performed by computers, the statute that has most impact on data processing security measures and controls is the Foreign Corrupt Practices Act of 1977—an amendment to the Securities and Exchange Act of 1934. The following presents pertinent parts of this significant law:

To begin with, its title is a misnomer. Its two main sections, *Accounting Standards* and *Foreign Corrupt Practices by Issuers,* affect *all* domestic and especially domestic public companies, as well as international corporations *that are subject to the Securities Exchange Act of 1934.* Specifically, through one of the Act's sections, entitled, *"Foreign Corrupt Practices by Domestic Concerns,"* the statute states that it applies to (a) any individual who is a citizen, national or resident of the U.S., (b) any corporation, partnership, association, joint-stock company, business, trust, unincorporated organization or sole proprietorship that has its principal place of business in the United States, or that is organized under the laws of a state, territory, possession or commonwealth of the United States.

5

Further, the *Accounting Standards* provision of the Act mandates that any company subject to the Securities Exchange Act of 1934 shall:

"(A) make and keep books, records, and accounts, which, in reasonable detail, accurately and fairly reflect the transactions and dispositions of the assets of the company; and

"(B) devise and maintain a system of internal accounting controls sufficient to provide reasonable assurances that—

"(i) transactions are executed in accordance with management's general or specific authorization;

"(ii) transactions are recorded as necessary (I) to permit preparation of financial statements in conformity with generally accepted accounting principles or any other criteria applicable to such statements, and (II) to maintain accountability for assets;

"(iii) access to assets is permitted only in accordance with management's general or specific authorization; and

"(iv) the recorded accountability for assets is compared with the existing assets at reasonable intervals and appropriate action is taken with respect to any differences."

Noncompliance of this Act can effect fines and jail sentences for offending directors and officers.

A hindsight note relating to a case in point: If the above Act had been enacted eight years earlier, perhaps it would have served as a deterrence for Stanley Goldblum, the youthful Chairman of the Board of Equity Funding Life Insurance Company (EFLIC), and his two close associates from perpetrating the $200 million computer-related fraud that was in operation from 1969 until March 30, 1973.

Human factor, in the form of a disgruntled ex-employee, Ronald Secrist (at one time an EFLIC Assistant Vice President), initiated the first crack in the highly polished computer-related scam. It seems that on March 7, 1973, Secrist, returning to the East Coast, contacted the Deputy Superintendent of the New York Insurance Department, who then telephoned Gleeson L. Payne, Insurance Commissioner of the State of California, about the top management of EFLIC being involved in writing and issuing large quantities of bogus policies.

The allegations were so "disturbing" that an investigation of EFLIC, which Payne earlier characterized as "one of the most efficiently run companies I know," and which was the "hottest stock" on the New York Stock Exchange began.

The genesis of Goldblum's computer-related fraud evolved from an interesting and, for a short time, highly successful idea: the Equity Funding Program. The concept, structured along the lines of the British Life Funding program and embellished by Goldblum, offered a highly salable and attractive combination of mutual funds and life insurance. Prospective customers were sold on the idea that by buying mutual fund shares, they could use the shares as collateral to purchase life insurance. Customers were assured that the dividends and appreciation of the mutual fund shares would pay for the insurance premiums and the interest on the borrowed amount.

However, the sales didn't come up to the expectation of the ambitious, enterprising, and highly sales-oriented Goldblum. To get a high volume of positive cashflow and an increased sales figure—both of which the company needed badly—Goldblum and his two associates came up with a "bold and creative" plan: issue fictitious life insurance policies for nonexisting people.

In carrying out the plan, records of the bogus policies were set up on the EFLIC computer as a subsystem, entitled "Department 99." This subsystem was partitioned from the company's other systems, and accessible via a complex password only to top management and the programmer, specially chosen for the job to design, develop, and maintain the "highly confidential system."

Actually, EFLIC used computer hardware and software to an extent that was rather uncommon if not unique in commercial enterprises in 1969. The company had the general ledger, journals, accounts receivable/accounts payable, payroll, inventory, "in-force" policies, sales commissions, and all other business transactions processed and stored by the computer.

The EFLIC triumvirate's theoretical concept became a high-production reality, and a large quantity of bogus policies were issued and then sold to reinsurers, i.e., other life insurance companies. Selling policies to reinsurers in order to spread actuarial risks and obtain cash is a normal practice in the insurance industry. Thus, EFLIC received 180 percent, the usual insurance commission, on nonexistent premiums. And because the policies were counterfeit, the company didn't have to pay out any sales commission or any other of the many expenses connected with issuing legitimate life insurance policies. In short, the money that EFLIC got from reinsurers for the bogus policies was clear profit.

But it was a short range windfall because of the life insurance industry's regulations. These regulations mandate that the company originating the policies has to turn 90 percent of the first year premiums from the policyholders over to the reinsurer. Thus, after a year of issuing bogus policies, EFLIC had to pay out cash for the fictitious policyholders. This, in turn, forced the cash-tight EFLIC, that is Goldblum et al, to generate more and more counterfeit insurance policies to be sold to reinsurers.

There was still another *creative* way EFLIC management generated cashflow: They took an appropriate number of fictious policyholders and simply put an end to their "computerized existence." The conspirators then filed with the reinsurers for death-benefit claims, labeling the sums they received as *current earnings* in the company's accounts.

In the meantime, the California Insurance Department and the Illinois Insurance Department (EFLIC, though headquartered in Studio City, California, was incorporated in Illinois) continued their examination of EFLIC's way of doing business.

As soon as word got out that examiners from two states were doing an in-depth audit of Equity Funding, stories of illegal opeations at EFLIC flooded Wall Street. The effect was predictable: Equity stock took a sharp decline on the New York Stock Exchange.

To counteract the rumors, Goldblum and one of his close associates flew to New York on Thursday, March 22, 1973. Goldblum gave several presentations to financial groups. He insisted that the states' auditing of his corporation's records was "a routine examination" and nothing more.

Notwithstanding all these last minute efforts, the order for seizure of the EFLIC company was served by the California Insurance Company at 6:30 PM Friday, March 30, 1973.

In April 1975, after the corporation went into bankruptcy under Chapter X, the forty-six year old Stanley Goldblum was sentenced to eight years at McNeil Island Federal Penitentiary, Washington. In addition, he was fined $20,000. While his two associates received seven years and five years respectively at different Federal Penitentiaries.

The Equity Funding caper, though it may not be "THE computer crime that started it all," as many computer experts claim, it certainly is one of the first computer-related frauds that gained national attention.

1.2 THE PRIVACY ACT OF 1974

Next in importance, insofar as management is concerned, is the Privacy Act of 1974. *Privacy*, as it relates to a collection of personal data, is very much a part of computer security. The Act involves the right of individuals to control or influence what information about them may be collected and stored, by whom, for what specific reasons, and to whom that information may then be disclosed.

The Privacy Act also covers the right of the individuals to know if information about them has been compiled, and if the said information is correct and complete. Furthermore, individuals have the right to challenge the accuracy of that information.

Technically, the Act is limited to government agencies and companies that work for them under contracts. However, the Act contains several provisions that are pertinent to computer security and possible computer crime at any DP facility.

For instance, the Act requires:

a. That each agency takes certain steps to maintain the security and confidentiality of records, and protects against any anticipated threats to security or integrity which could result in substantial harm, embarrassment, inconvenience, or unfairness to any individual on whom information is maintained.

b. That each agency accurately record disclosures of certain types of information under that agency's control.

c. That each agency establish "rules of conduct" for persons involved in the design, development, operation, or maintenance of any system or records involving personal data.

1.3 THE EXPORT ADMINISTRATION ACT OF 1979

The Export Administration Act of 1979 serves as a counter-measure against exporting without the proper license by restricting the sales of national security type equipment such as microchips, high technology equipment and systems (memory test systems, microwave receiver systems, micro-align semiconductor manufacturing devices, graphics plotting systems, and so on) to the USSR and the Warsaw Pact countries.

Case in point: Werner J. Bruchhausen, a young, handsome, six-foot West German national, between January, 1977, and June 5, 1980, illegally exported to the USSR and East Germany over $8 million and to West Germany over $2 million worth of the latest USA high technology devices.

How did Bruchhausen engineer such an operation? Rather than handle any of the details himself, he directed the profitable business through some "associates" he had set up in about half a dozen dummy corporations in California. His primary associates were an American, Anatoli (Tony) Maluta, also known as Tony Metz, and Sabina Dorn Tittle, another West German national.

As President of Bruchhausen's many and varied dummy corporations in this country, Maluta, assisted by Tittle, (Secretary-Treasurer) bought and shipped stolen Intel and Motorola microchips; bought under false pretenses and shipped with false licenses high technology devices such as a microwave receiver system from Watkins Johnson, a parallel operation memory test system from Fairchild, an Eclipse computer system from Data General; and so on and so on.

All the merchandise was exported to the USSR and Soviet bloc countries in falsely labeled boxes and without ever obtaining the required validated export license (which,

11

on account of the equipment being in the national security category, they would not have been able to get) from the U.S. Department of Commerce. Actually, to get around the Act, the products were shipped to Bruchhausen's dummy European firms in Vienna and Zurich. From these two Western European cities they were then rerouted to the USSR and East Germany by his overseas associates.

But then the human factor entered the picture: an executive of one of the high tech companies that Maluta was dealing with became suspicious, and he contacted the United States Department of Commerce. On August 19, 1981, after a year and a half of intensive investigation by R.W. Rice, special agent of Commerce, the Grand Jury indicted Bruchhausen and his co-conspirators on sixty counts. They were arrested and subsequently released on bail. The District Attorney who labeled Bruchhausen "high risk" did not want the man released, and agreed only after Bruchhausen's bail was set at $1,000,000. Events that followed proved just how right the District Attorney was in sizing up Bruchhausen.

On August 27, 1981, a bench warrant was issued for Bruchhausen who—the high bail notwithstanding—had left the country in great hurry by this date, and was seen in Europe enjoying the ambience of Monaco.

On December 7, 1981, Judge William Matthew Byrne, Jr., found both Maluta and Tittle guilty as charged. Maluta was sentenced for five years in federal prison and fined $60,000; while Tittle was sentenced for two years in federal prison and fined $10,000.

On January 25, 1982, Maluta and Tittle surrendered to the United States Marshall and began serving their sentences.

Another case in point: Proving that high technology smuggling is not restricted to one nationality, Gilles Gouzene, a 28-year-old French man, was arrested in February, 1984, by the U.S. Department of Commerce. Gouzene was charged with conspiracy and attempting to illegally export a Xynetics, Inc., $145,000 Model 200 Graphic Plotting System to an unnamed Eastern-bloc country.

The successful method used by Commerce to prevent this particular type of computer crime was an undercover "sting" operation that relied on the human factor: *greed*. Gouzene was looking for somebody who could arrange to ship the system illegally, yet not charge too much for such a service. It was at this point that the Commerce agents, acting as brokers, allegedly offered to get the "proper" export license for only $5,000. Thus the Commerce sting went into operation.

1.4 THE CALIFORNIA PENAL CODE

If the particular DP facility is in California, it behooves management to be aware of the following law when checking background security (see Chapter 6, Personnel Security) on a job applicant.

In California, adults who have been convicted of a crime but have served their sentence and have not clashed again with the law, can petition the court to have their conviction dismissed. And the court, according to the existing law, has to grant a dismissal, whether the crime was petty theft, grand larcency, or whatever. The fact is that the California Penal Code allows for the dismissal of just about any kind of conviction, with few exceptions.

Once dismissal is granted, the record is sealed and destroyed. Consequently, the person can then legally state in his application to a prospective employer that he has no criminal record.

1.5 STATES' COMPUTER CRIME LAWS

Management should be cognizant of the fact that twenty-three states—including California as of January 1, 1984—have enacted legislation stating that it is a crime to tamper with or steal from computer systems.

A computer fraud statute may not stop a professional embezzler such as Ross Eugene Fields (see Chapter 6, Personnel Security), but it should definitely deter DP personnel and end-users from committing computer-related fraud or embezzlement, or using the company's computer and programs for private business. Also, such legislation—if widely publicized—should put a damper on the young people who play "electronic invaders."

California's SB 835, being representative of such laws, is offered here as an example of state computer crime bills. In part, SB 835 reads as follows:

> "Any person who intentionally accesses or causes to be accessed any computer system or computer network for the purpose of (1) devising or executing any scheme or artifice to defraud or extort or (2) obtaining money, property, or services with false or fraudulent intent, representations, or promises, shall be guilty of a public offense.

> "Any person who maliciously accesses or causes to be accessed any computer system or computer network for the purpose of obtaining unauthorized information concerning the credit information of another person, or who introduces or causes to be introduced false information into that system or network for the purpose of wrongfully damaging or wrongfully enhancing the credit rating of any person shall be guilty of a public offense.

> "Any person who maliciously accesses, alters, deletes, damages, or destroys any computer system, computer network, computer program, or data, shall be guilty of a public offense."

Conviction carries a fine up to $5,000 and sixteen months in jail.

14

1.6 FEDERAL COMPUTER CRIME BILL

In June of 1984, the proposed Counterfeit Access Device and Computer Fraud and Abuse Act of 1984 (H.R. 5616) was approved by the U.S. House Judiciary Committee and was sent to the House of Representatives for consideration. It was expected to gain House and Senate approval quickly.

This crime bill was a swift reaction to a recent incident involving the theft of the password from a Sears Roebuck & Co. store in Sacramento—a subscriber of TRW, Inc.'s Information Services Division (a major credit bureau)—and a series of subsequent breaches of security by "hackers." The purpose of the *alleged* accesses to TRW's credit files of some ninety million people was credit card fraud.

The major provisions of the bill are:

1. H.R. 5616 applies to computers used by the Federal Government or used in interstate or foreign commerce, covering any system accessed by interstate telecommunications systems.

2. H.R. 5616 creates a specific federal felony for unauthorized access to computers if the defendant reaps $5,000 through computer fraud in one year, or if the defendant accesses classified information.

3. H.R. 5616 creates a misdemeanor crime of computer abuse if the defendant uses, modifies, or discloses information in a computer, and the defendant gains $5,000 or more in one year, or if the computer is operated by the Federal Government.

4. The penalty for misdemeanors is a $5,000 fine and up to one year in jail. The penalty for felonies is a $10,000 fine and up to ten years in jail.

5. Both the FBI and the Secret Service have jurisdiction over computer crime investigations under this legislation.

2

Establishing Computer Security

TWO
Establishing Computer Security

2.1 MANAGEMENT SECURITY PHILOSOPHY

The proliferation of microcomputers in offices and the increase of potential risks in computer fraud and abuse since most of the systems are on-line now sharpen the critical need for management to become involved in computer crime prevention and detection. Moreover, these counter-measures can best be effected if management formulates an effective security program that creates a climate of security.

To set up such a program, however, management has to be cognizant of the fact that while the constantly improving technologies provide good protection in physical, hardware, and software areas—as discussed in the following chapters—unless employees are security conscious, *computer abuse and other computer crimes are quite possible* in any organization. As to establishing a climate of security, it is the manager's responsibility to advise management that unless the company's security policy is directed not just at the DP department but at the whole enterprise, it is bound to fail.

Further, because the scope and effectiveness of a computer security program depends on proper management philosophy and support, management must have the following information to make the right decision: (1) an estimate, if not actual figures, of the value of the company's data and information in the computer and on tapes and disks; (2) an estimate on the possible loss of a vital system such as accounts receivable, inventory control, or payroll, due to an error or sabotage; and (3) an estimate of the possible loss in business interruption if a man-made or natural disaster occurs. In other words, management must be provided with a comprehensive risk analysis that assesses the risks in electronic data processing *throughout* the company.

However, if the security conscious DP manager happens to work in an organization where top management dismisses the possibility of computer crime and disasters as something that can happen to other organizations but "not to us," or where upper level management *is* aware of such possibilities but procrastinates in translating that awareness into supportive action, the following suggestions should help in getting support and money from management.

    a. Convince management via an effective presentation that they have a vested interest in computer crime detection and prevention methods, and of the necessity of placing appropriate value on critical company resources such as staff, data, and information, in addition to hardware and equipment.

    b. Persuade management to make a commitment for company-wide computer security. Such commitment might include approval to buy a security monitoring package such as CGA Software Products Group, Inc.'s *Top Secret,* Medium Systems Software and Services' *Secure,* IBM's *Resource Access Control Facility,* Electronic Data Systems Group's *Security Access Control,* a detection program such as

Blank's *Intruder Detection System,* and the like. (See discussion of commercial security packages in Chapter 5.)

Whether the company can afford a commercial package or not, the primary issue is to have management support an appropriate security system that balances technology with the human factor. More to the point, get management to subscribe to a computer security program that is based on the acknowledgement and appreciation of the fact that a *disgruntled employee* is a potential computer criminal; while a *satisfied employee* is the best deterrent a company can have against computer crime.

c. Convince management of the importance of having periodic but unannounced visits by external EDP auditors.

d. Ask management for authorization to control the number of desktop computer users in the company.

e. In the case of a large or even medium-size corporation, prevail upon management to set up a *computer security steering committee* (comprised of division and department heads and an internal EDP auditor) to consider and make recommendations to top management. Management can then make decisions on security measures based on the steering committee's recommendations *and* budget constraints. While in the case of a small company, explain to management that it is their responsibility to consider and decide upon the extent that the company can invest in computer crime detection and prevention methods.

f. Involve management in the establishment and maintainance of written computer security policies and standards, especially as they relate to personnel.

g. Assist management in making a decision as to what is the acceptable level of risk to the company—particularly if the company uses distributed data processing (DDP).

21

2.2 DIFFERENCE IN SECURITY APPROACHES FOR CENTRALIZED AND DISTRIBUTED DATA PROCESSING

Because a DDP environment poses significantly higher data security risks than a centralized mainframe environment, the approach to computer security in a DDP installation (whether a large or small site) has to be more "hard-nosed," IF it's to be effective.

In a centralized facility, for example, it is the computer security officer or the data base administrator who usually creates and controls the carefully designed passwords, the IDs, and authorization levels. In a DDP environment, however, management first has to decide and establish the degree of autonomy that each node in the company's DDP network may have. But autonomy notwithstanding, it is the responsibility of management to set up and enforce computer security procedures and to control standards to minimize, if not prevent, possible computer crimes—whether the DDP is comprised of mini, desktop, or personal computers, or whether the computers are scattered over a large territory or concentrated in one building. (These measures are to be implemented in addition to the internal hardware and software safeguards which are essential in both centralized and decentralized environments.)

Once the computer security standards are established in a DDP environment, it is up to the DP executive to police the nodes. To accomplish this he might assign a systems analyst to each node in the DDP network, and make him responsible for the integrity and security of that particular computer operation. The systems analyst would report to the DP manager but work hand-in-hand with the computer security officer—if there is one—creating passwords, IDs, and authorization levels. And the analyst would also work with the internal EDP auditor(s) insofar as input, exceptions, processing, audit trails, rejected items, and output controls are concerned.

In an environment where microcomputers access central data bases in a host computer, DP security must be subject to the same stringent physical, hardware, software, and personnel security measures as the structured DDP network.

2.3 RISK ANALYSIS

As stated before, it would be a mistake for management to approve the development of a security system or even to issue written security policies and standards, unless a risk analysis—based on a risk assessment that takes the human factor into account—has been undertaken and submitted to them. Since such risk analysis is essential in any type of computer facility, regardless of whether the company employs centralized or DDP systems, preparation of a risk analysis should be a mandatory prerequisite to setting up a computer security program.

But just what is a risk analysis?

Risk analysis is a systematic study that identifies and examines facility assets such as personnel, computer equipment and peripheral devices, proprietary software (if there are any), and electronically stores data and information. It also investigates areas vulnerable to natural or man-made disasters and criminal activities and estimates their possible loss in dollars. Finally, it identifies and reviews various safeguards, and then, based on cost/benefit analysis, it recommends the most effective, albeit affordable, countermeasures. The following is a suggested guide to conduct risk analysis.

a. Evaluate all hardware in terms of replacement costs, processing-interruption costs, and the costs of obtaining temporary outside hardware.

b. Define the volume and the dollar value of all computer systems, applications, and programs that contain corporate or, as the case may be, government agency information; systems that process financial data, such as EFT (electronic funds transfer) and EFT-based applications including ATM (automatic teller machine), POS (point-of-sale) terminals, telephone banking services, automated clearinghouses, cash management services, and MMIS (Medicaid Management Information System), welfare, and similar government paid funds.

c. Evaluate the above and all other systems that contain sensitive data in terms of business-interruption costs, third party liability, and the costs of obtaining outside DP services to process urgent business and company data and information.

d. Define the staff positions that need high level authorization to access sensitive data; estimate the loss in case of possible fraud or embezzlement involving such sensitive data, and ensure that people with high level authorization *are aware* of the study *and* its result.

Case in point: Stanley Slyngsted, an information supervisor at the Department of Social and Health Services in Olympia, Washington, defrauded the state with some $17,000 between April 1982 and March 1983 by issuing checks to himself. Slyngsted was able to commit the computer crime because he designed the program that issued the particular payments, using the agency's Sperry Corporation's

24

Model 1100/82 mainframe. Moreover, as a supervisor, he had constant access to the program and the data the program used.

Slyngsted, though clever in destroying audit trails of his embezzlement, was caught through the canceled checks that were made out to different names but bore the same address: Slyngsted's.

In July 1983 Slyngsted was sentenced to ten years in Federal Prison by Thurston County Superior Court Judge, Hewitt Henry.

Hindsight note: Considering human frailties, it is doubtful that Slyngsted would have risked his position to engage in criminal activities if the agency would have conducted a security review periodically or, if they would have had a policy of not allowing the person who designs a program to run the same.

The fact of the matter is that a risk analysis that includes step "d" can be an effective deterrent in computer crimes like the above.

e. Analyze fraud potentials in vulnerable systems and applications. For example, in an ATM application the following fraud potentials may exist:

1. Illegal transaction through the use of lost or stolen magnetic card and possibly PIN (personal identification number).

2. Forced entry into the ATM.

3. False issuance of ATM card and PIN by program modification.

4. Misappropriation of magnetic card and PIN by staff (stolen at work).

5. Illegal savings withdrawal via falsification of ATM account.

6. Wiretap to falsify accounts, attain PIN, or falsely order ATM withdrawals.

7. Fictitious request for ATM card and PIN.

8. Natural disasters such as fire, flood, and the like.

When the fraud potentials are defined, the expected annual loss should be compiled. Figure 1 is an example of such a chart in an ATM application.

f. Assume the role of the devil's advocate. For example, try on an on-line VDT (video display terminal) to access sensitive data in a particular computer sys-

EXPECTED ANNUAL LOSS

Risk from Above	Estimated Yearly Occurrence	Estimated X Dollar Loss = per Occurrence	Annual Expected Loss
1	16	x 200 limit/ withdrawal =	3,200
2	.25	x 4000 cash limit/ATM =	1,000
3	.25	x 6200 limit/ month =	1,550
4	4	x 6200 =	24,800
5	1	x 6200 =	6,200
6	.25	x 4000 =	1,000
7	10	x 6200 =	62,000
8	.25	x 4000 cash 100 from lost receipts =	1,250

TOTAL ANNUAL
EXPECTED LOSS
IN DOLLARS $101,000

Through the courtesy of Albert L. Miller, Security Analyst

FIGURE 1

tem *without* proper authorized access codes. Or, try to make unauthorized programming changes and see if the current system safeguards will detect it. Or, try to penetrate the existing computer room security by having an unauthorized person enter the area.

g. Once the vulnerable areas are defined, and the likelihood and costs of possible sabotage or computer fraud determined, these factors are matched against the cost/benefit of a proposed security system. The following cost/benefit analysis example (Figure 2) is part of the previously introduced ATM risk analysis.

h. Last but not least, management—based on factors presented in the risk analysis—has to decide upon the scope and extent of computer crime countermeasures (including EDP insurance) *after* establishing the dollar value of losses acceptable to the company.

COST/BENEFIT ANALYSIS

Item	Capital Investment/ Start-up Costs	Annual Operating Costs	Annual Loss Avoidance
Crytographic Equipment	12,000	————	1,000
PIN Forms	————	1,600	1,600
ATM Card Warning Forms	————	1,000	1,600
ATM Lighting	3,000	100	500
Video Surveillance	4,800	300	500
Special Printer for PIN Issuance	1,000	200	21,700
Printer and Terminal for ATM Card Issuance	1,300	————	21,700
Change to computer OS for Security Logs and PIN's	–?–	–?–	37,400

COST/BENEFIT ANALYSIS (cont.)

Item	Capital Investment/ Start-up Costs	Annual Operating Costs	Annual Loss Avoidance
Additional Personnel	----	15,000	10,750
Existing Security	----	----	----
Burglar Alarm	----	----	4,250
TOTAL	$22,100	$18,200	$101,000

$$\text{Expected Annual Return on Expenditures for Countermeasures} = \frac{101,000 - 18,200}{18,200} \times 100 = 455\%$$

(excludes costs associated with the generation of security logs and batch totals)

Through the courtesy of Albert L. Miller, Security Analyst

FIGURE 2

2.4 RISK MANAGEMENT

Risk management is the logical and proper continuation of risk analysis, and it is usually the responsibility of the computer security manager/officer. Proper risk management implements and maintains the accepted security recommendations, and ensures that the established computer crime countermeasures and DP controls are enforced in all the vulnerable areas. The person in charge might enforce risk management in the following way:

a. By periodically re-evaluating the effectiveness of the installed physical, hardware, software, and personnel security measures and controls, as well as their costs.

b. By instituting well thought out education seminars to effect proper security awareness at both management and staff levels.

c. By conducting annual security briefings of staff who have a high authorization level.

d. By communicating as effectively as possible to all personnel the significance of being committed to security on an individual basis.

2.5 SECURITY POLICY AND STANDARDS MANUALS

Simple, well written security policy and standards manuals convey to the reader the importance of adhering to management policies and standards, thus serving as a possible deterrent for computer crime. Such documents—which, by the way, should be printed in limited numbers and have *controlled distribution*—may consist of the following:

a. The *objective* of each manual is to be presented in clear, concise language. For example, "The objective of this manual is to communicate to all levels of staff the Company's computer security policy insofar as prevention and detection of computer crime is concerned."

b. The *approach* used in each section of a particular manual to accomplish the defined objectives is to be stated simply. For example, "We will define—according to the established standards—the backup and recovery procedures. This is to minimize the impact of errors, accidents, disasters, theft, fraud, and sabotage, if any of these events occurs."

c. The *resources* such as hardware, software, data, information, supplies, and so on, which are to be described in a general way and not in detail. (A definitive description of computer data and information resources—all of which are highly confidential—is to be on a tape, which is backed up, periodically up-dated, stored, and accessed only by a few designated people.)

d. The *possible threats* against the stated resources, and the security measures and controls the company is instituting to counter them, which are to be listed clearly, concisely.

e. *The management and staff positions* that top man-agement designated to administer the approved com-puter security policies and standards, which are to be defined. For example, "The DP manager has the prime responsibility for securing and maintaining the protection of the company's data and informa-tion resources. He is also responsible for issuing ap-propriate procedures to obtain compliance with the established policies."

2.6 UPDATING PROCEDURES

Insofar as security policy and standards manuals are con-cerned, it is crucial that proper updating procedures are es-tablished and enforced. If, for example, there is a change in management philosophy—whether due to new top man-agement or outside economic or other factors—a change in security policy is quite likely. And, if there is a drastic change in the type of data processing system being used, such as converting from a centralized DBMS to a DDP net-work, or changing from COBOL to Fortran or to a fourth generation language, a change in the programming and pro-cessing standards is inevitable. Finally, there are also minor, nonetheless noteworthy, modifications to existing security policies and standards that require updating.

The actual mechanism for proper updating may be nothing more than a simple, self-explanatory UPDATING LOG form, such as the following example (see Figure 3).

SAMPLE UPDATING LOG

INSTRUCTIONS: New pages will be issued as necessary. Please update the manual by removing the obsolete page, and replacing it with the new page.

For each update, enter the date received as well as the page number.

#	Date	Page #		#	Date	Page #
1				21		
2				22		
3				23		
4				24		
5				25		
6				26		
7				27		
8				28		
9				29		
10				30		
11				31		
12				32		
13				33		
14				34		
15				35		
16				36		
17				37		
18				38		
19				39		
20				40		

FIGURE 3

However, to ensure that the updating log's "instructions" are adhered to, the computer security officer or DP manager is to periodically spot-check manuals within the controlled distribution. Use Figure 4 for the Checklist.

RISK ANALYSIS CHECKLIST

Analyst: (Name)			*Date:*
Procedures Performed	*Yes*	*No*	*Comments (if "no" is checked)*
Identification and evaluation of all facility assets			
Definition of the volume and $$ statistics of vital systems & applications			
Evaluation of the above + all other business-sensitive systems			
Definition of high level authorization staff positions			
Analysis of fraud potentials in vulnerable systems & applications			
Determination of possible penetration of computer security			
Compilation of possible expected annual loss			
Cost/Benefit Analysis			

FIGURE 4

32

3

Physical
Security

THREE
Physical Security

Once management has given its support and direction for computer crime countermeasures, the DP manager is ready to set up physical security, which in terms of human factors is the first line of prevention and detection against unlawful or forced entry into a DP facility.

In addition, given that adherence to the basic principles of physical security in establishing hardware, software, and personnel security can provide the accountability that effects a climate of security, it has to be carefully planned, implemented, and maintained.

Full range of physical security may consist of some or all of the following measures, depending upon the size and type of DP facility the company is operating.

3.1 BUILDING AND PARKING LOT SECURITY

If it is a large DP center, physical security starts with the building and its parking lot. Specifically, it should include:

a. Well lighted entrance and parking lot at night.

b. No signs to advertise the fact that the building houses a DP facility.

c. No windows on the first two floors of the DP center.

Fact is that because of several violent acts in the past, most the DP centers built or remodeled the last six to eight years have solid walls on the first two floors. In addition, many DP facilities on upper floors use laminated windows so that nobody can look into the building from the outside, not even if you are a window cleaner on a scaffold.

d. Security guards patrolling the parking lot at regular intervals, especially in the evening and at night, given that for financial reasons most large DP centers operate 24 hours a day.

If the DP facility is small or only one of the departments of the company, it makes good sense to have it located on an upper floor, if possible. However, whether the DP facility occupies the whole building or only a floor, to ensure the prevention and detection of unauthorized persons in the area, stationing security guards in the lobby is a *must*.

The next step in establishing physical security is *access control:* a critical factor in deterring computer crime.

3.2 PHYSICAL ACCESS CONTROL

To prevent unauthorized persons from entering the computer facility, the following measures are essential:

3.2.1 Magnetic ID and badges

The encoded magnetic-strip ID cards or badges of DP personnel as well as consultants (on contract or temporary assignment) entering the facility are to be checked by security guards. In the case of consultants, the ID cards are to be scrutinized carefully to see if they are valid. (Still a better method to ensure that no ex-employee or consultant enters the DP facility is to ask for the ID card/badge when an employee terminates or is terminated, or when a consultant is finished with his assignment.)

Case in point: Stanley Mark Rifkin, a soft-spoken, pleasant computer consultant from Sepulveda, California, defrauded the Security Pacific Bank in Los Angeles of $10.2 million via EFT on October 25, 1978.

The short, pudgy consultant was able to commit one of the most imaginative computer-related crimes of that year because the security guard did not check Rifkin's ID card when he flashed it on entering the bank's DP center lobby that afternoon. The fact of the matter was that as of May 1978 Rifkin was no longer working on an assignment to the bank, and consequently his ID card was invalid.

Once past the security guard, Rifkin walked directly to the wire transfer room where, during his previous assignment to design an alternate system to the bank's computer processed EFT system, he spent some time. In fact, it was while he observed first hand the procedures and operations of the wire transfer room that Rifkin got the idea of robbing the bank via the very system he was paid to protect by developing and implementing a backup system.

At the door of the wire transfer room he identified himself to the staff, and told him that he was on another assignment to study "how the system could be improved." The operator remembered him, and Rifkin had no trouble in entering the highly sensitive area.

Thus unopposed, Rifkin walked around the room with a notebook in his hand, jotting down several data *including* the secret transfer code of the day displayed in plain view on the wall.

In those days, the bank officials were very careful in changing the code daily (the EFT ID password) that was used by authorized upper level management for transferring large sums of money from one branch to another, from one bank to another, here and worldwide. However, they neglected to follow up on their security measure in the most important part of the EFT operations: the wire transfer room. They failed to take the human factor into consideration and inform the supervisor of the high risk factor of the code and the importance of giving the highly confidential code to authorized personnel only.

Having obtained the data he came for, Rifkin waved goodby to the busy staff and walked out of the bank. Out on the street he went to the nearest pay telephone booth and called the wire transfer room which he just left.

When the EFT operator answered, Rifkin gave the day's secret transfer code, and then, pretending to be an executive from the International Department of the bank, he instructed the operator to transfer $10.2 million to Wozchod Handelsbank, a Swiss bank, in Zurich, Switzerland. He told the operator that the stated amount was to be credited to the account of one, Russalmaz Agency, in Geneva, Switzerland.

Next morning, Rifkin flew from the Los Angeles International Airport to Geneva, Switzerland, where—through a Los Angeles diamond broker—he met the Soviet wholesale diamond agency's managing director. Rifkin wanted to buy diamonds, which he believed were highly salable commodities, for the full $10.2 million he stole. However, the Russian agency had only $8,145,000 worth of diamonds to sell.

When Russalmaz Agency's bank received the proper amount, the ever cautious Russians did not hand over the diamonds. Instead, they gave Rifkin a claim ticket for a piece of baggage to be picked up at the duty-free Geneva airport.

Next day, before boarding an airplane back to the states via Frankfurt, Germany, and with a stop-over at Luxembourg, Rifkin retrieved an unmarked canvas bag with the claim ticket. Then without opening it, he entrusted it to the flight attendant to ensure that it would go on the same flight with him.

In Luxembourg, Rifkin, accompanied by his expensive luggage and the contrasting shabby canvas bag, took a taxi to the best hotel in town. In the hotel room, Rifkin locked the doors securely, gently placed the bulky bag on the bed, and then opened it and emptied it slowly. Some $8.2 million worth of polished diamonds, like sparkling champagne, cascaded upon the dark red velvet bedcover.

After an appropriate period of admiration, Rifkin folded the empty canvas bag and placed it on the bottom of his expensive leather luggage. Next, he put the tightly re-packed diamonds in a transparent travel clothes container under a couple of neatly folded dress shirts, and closed his suitcase.

The following morning the euphoric Rifkin boarded a plane for New York City where, according to his carefully worked out plan, he was to embark on the next stage of his becoming an instant millionaire. At the John F. Kennedy airport, however, he had a few tense moments when he had to go through Customs. But the Customs officials had no reason to turn over every piece of Rifkin's neatly packed suitcase, and so they missed the diamonds.

From New York, Rifkin flew to Rochester where he tried to prevail upon an old friend to open and run a wholesale diamond brokerage in New York City for him. Rifkin's story was that he just came back from Europe where he was involved in a large real-estate operation, and that his share of the profit was paid mostly in polished diamonds and only partly in currency.

To convince his friend that he was serious about the deal, Rifkin gave the man $6,000 in cash. However, while the old friend was thinking over the attractive offer, the theft was discovered by Security Pacific Bank officials, and the FBI was called in to find Rifkin *and* the stolen millions.

News of the theft together with a picture of the fugitive Rifkin was featured on the 11 o'clock evening TV news on November 3, 1978. Rifkin's friend happened to see the broadcast. Not wanting to be involved in any criminal activity he immediately called Security Pacific Bank officials in Los Angeles, and then contacted the chief FBI agent in Rochester. But Rifkin too saw the broadcast as he was ready to get into bed in his hotel room, and he took the next plane out of Rochester back to California.

His flight was to no avail however. On November 7, 1978 Rifkin was arrested in Carlsbad, California, at the home of another unsuspecting friend.

On March 26, 1979, the Honorable William Matthew Byrne, Jr., Judge, in Los Angeles, sentenced Stanley Mark Rifkin to eight years in a Federal Prison of which he served less than three years before being released.

Hindsight note: This computer-related theft could have been deterred with a few simple but effective procedures such as:

   a. Better access control in the lobby of the bank's DP center.
   b. Prohibiting former consultants, or for that matter former employees, to hold on to their ID cards or badges.
   c. Better access control to the wire transfer room in the form of an electronic device that uses magnetic-strip cards to activate the door, and not permitting any outsider to enter the room without a written authorization by the organization's security officer.

d. Better security controls for the daily changed EFT transfer code by giving it to the supervisor only. The supervisor then can pass it on in *confidence* to the operator on duty. In addition, the wire transfer room can have a policy to call back the person who is asking the operator to transfer money *before* those orders are carried out.

3.2.2 Visitors' ID

Visitors should be given a visitor's badge and asked to sign the log book, specifying the DP employee they are visiting, as well as the date and the time of their arrival. Moreover, the DP staff (or his secretary) is to come and get the visitor in the lobby, and act as an escort. A cardinal rule of effective computer crime deterrence is that a visitor may not go anywhere in the DP facility unless accompanied by a DP staff. When a visitor leaves the DP facility, he is to *return* his temporary badge and record in the log book the time of his departure.

3.2.3 Facility access

Within the facility, areas that contain sensitive information such as the computer room, data library, I/O rooms, and wire transfer room (in banks and other financial institutions) should be accessible only to authorized personnel. Moreover, these areas, and especially the computer room are to be equipped with a *single entry door* (not counting the emergency doors) and electronic door lock. The electronic device on each door can be activated only with the appropriate encoded magnetic-strip ID card. The device also automatically logs the ID number and the time a person enters the particular room.

3.2.4 Intrusion detection devices

Devices such as cameras or closed-circuit televisions should be used to monitor the entrances of sensitive and high risk areas to guard against access by unauthorized personnel.

41

3.3 FIRE SECURITY/PROTECTION

Since fire is the most frequent cause of damage and loss in computer centers according to insurance companies, the greater the attention paid to fire protection, the less risk involved, and the less insurance premium the company has to pay. The following text lists effective fire prevention measures for most, if not all, DP installations.

3.3.0.1 All walls, floors, and ceilings of the DP facility should have a minimum two-hour fire rating.

3.3.0.2 Tape, record, and documentation safes should have a mimimum of four-hour fire rating.

3.3.0.3 Access doors to the outside (in case of emergency) should have automatic panic-hardware equipped and self-closing devices. No entrance to the computer room or the tape library from the *outside* is to be provided.

3.3.0.4 Fire alarm should be wired so that it rings simultaneously at the DP facility and the nearest fire department.

3.3.0.5 Fire alarm signals should be located where prompt response is assured, such as in well-traveled corridors, coffee room, and the like.

3.3.0.6 Fusible link actuated fire dampers (utilizing an easily melted metal such as lead) should be used to close all heating and air-conditioning ducts in the computer room.

3.3.0.7 Rooms and vaults used for storing backup tapes and records in case of destruction of the primary data should be located in a separate building at sufficient distance, so that minimal loss of data occurs in case of disaster. But the separately located storage rooms or vaults are to have one-hour fire rated walls, floors, and ceilings also. And, in addition, are also to be protected by an automatic nondamaging fire-extinguishing system.

3.3.0.8 Automatic sprinkler systems should be installed throughout the supply rooms and support areas. To prevent water damage, which can be very costly, sufficient number of polyethylene covers are to be provided.

3.3.0.9 Automatic smoke and ionization detection systems should be installed in the ceiling of the computer room, and a water detection system (in case the air conditioning unit breaks down) should be installed under the *raised* floor.

3.3.0.10 Halon or some similar system should be installed throughout the computer room. (Halon is a DuPont trade name for an extinguishing agent that controls fire but does not damage the machines nor does it displace oxygen. It mixes with oxygen. Some authorities claim that Halon forms poisonous gas; while other authorities are just as emphatic in stating that Halon is harmless. Most DP facilities, to be on the safe side, direct all persons to leave the premisis BEFORE Halon is activated.) The gaseous system requires detection system actuation and automatic interlocking with air conditioning and computer power to maintain gas concentration and remove the source of electrical ignition.

3.3.0.11 Smoke detection and Halon or some similar system should be provided for under the floor areas in the tape library and wire transfer room (if there is one).

3.4 HOUSEKEEPING IN COMPUTER AND STORAGE ROOMS

Borrowing a term from programming, housekeeping in this sense means procedures that contribute to proper fire prevention measures in the computer and storage areas.

3.4.0.1 Records, paper supplies, spare tape and disk packs or other combustibles in the computer room should be limited to the working minimum needed for daily requirement.

3.4.0.2 Smoking, drinking, and eating in the computer room and data storage area should be prohibited.

3.4.0.3 Self-closing lid waste cans for paper and other combustible trash should be provided in the computer and data storage rooms.

3.5 AIR-CONDITIONING SYSTEM

Because large mainframes are sensitive to temperature and humidity variations, there should be control devices on the air conditioning units that monitor such fluctuations. If an unacceptable condition should occur, the control devices can trigger an alarm.

In addition, the air ducts of the air conditioning units should be secured against access (burglary or gas bomb) by heavy-gauge screens, and the air intake is to be monitored by a special device for gaseous substances.

In a distributed data processing environment that is composed of mini- and/or microcomputers, there is no need for special air conditioning. Nevertheless, extreme heat or cold will affect these small computers. Consequently, such conditions are to be guarded against by temperature control.

3.5.0.1 Master controls for utilities such as electric power, lights, air conditioner, and water should be located in controlled access areas.

3.5.0.2 Emergency lighting for safe evacuation in case of fire or other disaster should be provided in all areas of the DP facility.

4

Hardware Security

FOUR
Hardware Security

The second component in establishing total security for the deterrence, protection, and detection of computer crime with the human factor in mind is hardware security. The importance of protecting the items within this category cannot be overemphasized.

4.1 ELECTRIC POWER

Since computer operations are totally dependent on constant and clean electric power, not to mention the company's substantial investment in computer equipment, it is imperative to use every possible means to shield the electric power supply from possible sabotage by disgruntled employees or outside terrorists. The following presents possible methods and measures toward that goal:

4.1.1 UPS (uninterruptible power supply) system

Whether designed for mainframes, mini- or microcomputers, UPS is a reliable standby power source *if* manufactured by a reputable firm. It is used for protection against deliberate or accidental blackouts and brownouts, as well as power-line anomalies such as electrical noises and voltage sags—the most frequent causes of system malfunctions and computer errors.

Until rather recently UPS, consisting of a rectifier, an inverter, and a static switch, was a large piece of equipment that was too bulky and noisy to be located in the computer room. Now, however, most manufacturers of UPS systems are using high technology power transistors resulting in products that are small, quiet, *and* more efficient, and can be placed next to the mainframe or mini-computer in the computer room. Moreover, the new transistorized UPS systems are rechargeable, and can generally provide up to thirty five minutes (some particular models even longer) of power to sustain DP operations through a blackout or brownout. And finally, because the transistorized UPS system consists of few parts, they hardly need any servicing.

4.1.2 Off-site Backup Power Service

In addition to UPS, off-site backup power service is another necessary security measure. Granted it is quite expensive, but for large DP operations it can save the company hundreds of thousands of dollars in case of prolonged power failure. The backup can be an off-site commercially available power service or an off-site company-built power generator. In either case, the backup emergency power switches on automatically, thus providing electric power to the facility's central processing unit so that the company's computer operations can continue without interruption.

4.2 TERMINALS

Without a doubt terminals, whether local or remote, stand-alone or mainframe-connected, dumb or intelligent, type-writer or video display type, are the most vulnerable devices in today's on-line computer systems, bar none.

Taking into account the risks that terminals represent, in addition to ID and authorization level-based passwords to the users, hardware security against possible unauthorized use of terminals is to be enforced. Existing computer crime deterrence and detection terminal techniques include the following:

4.2.0.1 Terminal lock and key is the simplest to use but the easiest to penetrate. The user inserts the correct key into the lock, turns the key, and the terminal is ready for use.

If terminal lock and key are used, the user must understand that *he is responsible* if anybody gets hold of his key and uses the terminal for theft or abuse of programs, records, or data.

4.2.0.2 Magnetic-strip card is more expensive than lock and key, but much more effective. The user inserts the card into a terminal-connected magnetic card reader and the encoded ID is verified by a control file. If the verification is positive, the terminal is switched on. If the verification is negative, the terminal remains shut off. It cannot be used.

Nevertheless, because people are prone to leave their magnetic-strip cards next to the terminal or on their desk, or lose them, they must understand that they are responsible if any unauthorized person is using their terminal.

4.2.0.3 Fingerprint and palm print, which works something like this: the user places his finger or palm in a hand-shaped electronic device attached to the terminal. The sensors-read finger or palm print is matched and verified by a control file. Again, if the verification is positive, the terminal is switched on. If the verification is negative, the terminal remains shut off.

4.2.0.4 Signature analysis and voice print, which, according to some experts, are at least as accurate if not more so than finger or palm prints. In the first instance, either the complete signature, or the signature initiation impulse time is compared and verified by a control file. In the second instance, the person speaks certain words into a terminal-attached microphone, and the electronically converted voice message is matched and verified by a control file. A positive verification switches the terminal on; a negative verification leaves the terminal in a shut-off state.

4.3 DATA COMMUNICATIONS/NETWORK LINES

Because of the trend toward distributed data processing and the mushrooming of microcomputers in company offices and homes that have networking capabilities, not to mention EFT (electronic funds transfer) system applications such as the ubiquitous ATM (automatic teller machines), and others, data security in telecommunications has become a high priority topic for DP as well as non-DP executives. Moreover, because under the Privacy Act of 1974, as discussed in Chapter 1, personal and confidential data must be safeguarded by organizations, there is an increased need for protecting not only proprietary but other sensitive data as well during transmission.

At present, the only known practical means of deterring possible wiretappers from stealing data and information transmitted over various communications media is data encryption or cryptography.* Data encryption systems scramble transmitted data, so that if intercepted, they are incomprehensible and consequently useless to the computer criminal.

4.3.1 Encryption Systems

Before discussing the various encryption systems, consisting of an encryptor with appropriate software to interface with a modem (a modulator and demodulator device), perhaps a definition data encryption is in order.

Data encryption is the precise process or algorithm (see definition in cipher systems below) through which the original intelligible data—called *plain text*—is converted to an unintelligible sequence of numbers or symbols, called *cipher text*. The reverse process or algorithm through which the cipher text is converted back to plain (understandable) text is called *data decryption*.

4.3.2 Code Systems versus Cipher Systems.

The two methods to convert data from one form to another are code systems and cipher systems.

4.3.2.1 Code systems (used by the military for ages) require a code book to transform plain text to cipher text. Consequently, this method is quite limited because of the number of codes that can be used.

---

*The word cryptography, by the way, comes from two Greek words: *kryptos*, meaning hidden, and *graphein*, meaning to write.

4.3.2.2 Cipher systems require a cryptographic algorithm, which is a definitive set of computational procedures that resolves a problem or performs a mathematical transformation within a finite number of structured steps, *and* a key or keys to transform plain text to cipher text and vice versa. Now a "key" is a specific combination or pattern of characters or bits that serves as a secret parameter or sequence of numbers used in a given algorithm.

However, as sophisticated as cryptosystems are, no encryption method is stronger than the protection given to the keys. This points to the necessity of seeing to it that the more conventional prevention and detection methods are in place as well. Such methods, as stated before, include a realistic evaluation of risks in any and all types of data processing throughout the organization, with special consideration given for the role of human factors in potential computer crimes. In other words, if *all* aspects of a total computer security system are not implemented and maintained appropriately, the most sophisticated encryption techniques will not prevent possible *cryptanalysis*—the name by which the illegal code-breaking, by wire-fraud experts, is known.

4.3.3 DES (Data Encryption Standard) versus PKE (Public Key Encryption).

Two approaches are available in cipher systems to encrypt data: the private key used in DES, and the public key used in PKE.

4.3.3.1 The private key approach used in the DES algorithm-based cipher system consists of *one* secret conversion key that *encrypts* data sent over a public channel such as cable, microwave, fibre-optics, satellite, and the like. The same single key is then relayed to the authorized receiver over a secured channel such as unlisted, private telephone, or sent by a courier. Subsequently, the receiver *decrypts* the data.

DES—established by the National Bureau of Standards in 1977 as the United States Federal encryption algorithm standard, and adopted by ANSI (American National Standards Institution) in 1980 for commercial use—employs the private key approach (Figure 5).

Because DES, a strong cryptographic algorithm—coupled with S-box, the hardware (encryptor) that implements it—uses block encryption to transform a stream of input bits of fixed-length plain text into a stream of output bits of different fixed-length cipher text, and because through DES algorithm there are 72 quadrillion possible keys (possible combinations of parameters or sequence of numbers), it is being used in EFT systems applications. DES's image is enforced by cryptography experts who claim that it would take a hundred years or so for a wiretapper to figure out the 72 quadrillion possible key combinations. It remains to be seen if any cryptanalyst will challenge this statement.

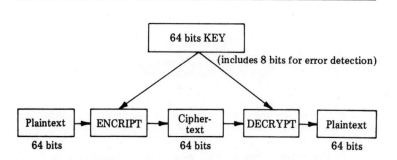

FIGURE 5 DES, The Private Key Approach

4.3.3.2 The public key approach used in PKE algorithm-based cipher system consists of *two* separate keys that are used at the transmitting and at the receiving stations (Figure 6). Each user has a deciphering key which he keeps secret, and an enciphering key which is in the public domain.

The published key can be used by any user to encipher another person's data. However, only the person who knows the secret key of the particular user can convert cipher text (encrypted data) into plain text (decrypted data). An example of the public key approach is key management system which uses the RSA algorithm—named after its inventors: Rivest, Shamir, and Adleman.

In key management system, a certain number of users communicate with each other. Each user defines his own

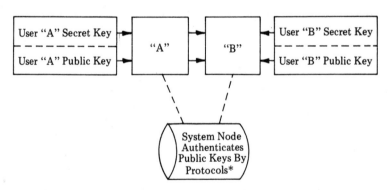

*Protocols are pre-determined set of conventions covering the format and timing of messages between two communicating processes.

FIGURE 6 PKE, The Public Key Approach

secret and public key. The public keys then are stored at a system node (the key distribution center) for authentication. Thus, when User (a) is ready to communicate with User (b) he sends his *public key* and the *public key* of User (b).

The key distribution center authenticates both keys. Then, after several handshake protocols* between the sending and the receiving public keys, User (a), who was given the secret key by User (b), and User (b), who was given the secret key by User (a), can start to have a meaningful conversation.

4.3.4 Commercially available encryptors.

There are several manufacturers, including IBM, Analytics, Racal-Milgo, Inc., Paradyne Corp., and others, that offer DES and PKE algorithm-based encryption systems.

Normally, these encryption devices are rather easy to operate, after minimal training by the vendor, and currently they average under $5,000 per link. However, it is quite possible in today's high technology competition that encryptors will be even more reasonable in the future.

Given that, today, high volumes of valuable and confidential data and information are being transmitted over different communications media, and that there is the possibility of cryptanalysts waiting "in the wings," trying to steal profitable data, it behooves top management to use encryption and/or other available or developing technology for the deterrence and prevention of computer crime in a high risk situation: during transmission.

---

*Protocols are a set of conventions governing the format and timing of messages between two communicating processes.

4.3.5 MAC (Message Authentication Code) versus Voice Verification System.

The following techniques are only two of the many up-coming methods that are being developed to protect the integrity of EFT systems from computer criminals:

4.3.5.1 In **MAC,** cryptographic check digits are appended to the message as to its transaction type, transaction account number, destination, point of origin, and identification information. Consequently, messages without such additional check digits are rejected. Also, MAC provides the means by which valid transactions cannot be modified without detection.

MAC, in conjunction with DES or PKE cryptographic algorithms, may best be utilized in EFT when it is implemented within a hardware security module. The module can be self-contained, physically secure, microprocessor controlled, and security device programmed to perform all the cryptographic functions. It can be a DP peripheral device that interfaces with the organization's DP systems. The interfacing can be accomplished by the computer sending sensitive data or information directly to the module to perform its functions.

By this method, the information sent as well as the keys used in encrypting the information are never in the clear. Moreover, the hardware module can be secured by both physical locks and interlock circuitry, so that all the information that has to be transformed from plain text to cipher text is within the module. Additionally, no matter how this module is opened—whether legitimately by two physical keys entrusted to two people or forced open—the built-in interlock circuitry causes all data stored in the module, such as cryptographic keys, to be erased.

4.3.5.2 The voice verification system on the other hand is based (obviously) on voice recognition. A pioneer in this field is Threshold Technology, Inc., Delran, New Jersey, which invented a speech-recognition algorithm that identifies a work regardless of the identity of the speaker by recognizing basic phonetic patterns.

Threshold's latest speaker-recognition system, which associates the sound of a particular word with a particular speaker, was chosen by a large bank in Chicago for their EFT system. Since this bank transfers approximately $30 billion of corporate deposits daily on the basis of telephoned requests, they mandated that the system "must be impervious to unauthorized access."

Threshold's speaker-recognition system works something like this:

The system, using a word-recognition algorithm that works on isolated words instead of continuous speech, randomly selects four words for the caller to say. The caller has four chances to respond correctly to four different sets of words.

If the response is correct and the user's voice is verified, the funds-transfer process begins. If the user's response is correct but his voice is unverifiable or if his response is incorrect, he is unable to access and use the funds-transfer program.

5

Software Security

FIVE
Software Security

Two of the least publicized yet most common computer crimes that impact industry and government to the tune of millions of dollars annually are the theft and copying of software and data. Looking at this phenomenon from the human factor viewpoint, it is quite clear that DP employees who succumb to the temptation to steal and/or copy valuable software and data for sale or to do a favor for a friend, are doing it simply because they know that they can get away with it. If effective computer crime countermeasures are set up, published, *and* disseminated throughout the company, employees will get the clear message that detection of their "profitable side-line" and subsequent prosecution for such activities are real possibilities. Consequently, they will think twice before attempting any type of *software piracy* regardless of how much the company's competitor, a government behind the iron curtain, or just a businessman who wants to save a lot time, money, and effort, is offering them for a particular software or data.

The many deterrence, prevention, control, and detection methods currently in use to protect computer software and data against potential computer criminals are detailed below.

A fundamental deterrence against theft and copying of software and data and other DP crime methods (see section 5.4) is the presence of an internal EDP auditor *plus* the periodic visits of an external EDP auditor. Generally, the internal auditor's responsibility is to monitor the adequacy and effectiveness of controls in computer systems: review and appraise DP applications; assist the external EDP auditor; and prepare management reports. While the external auditor's responsibility is to periodically check for any weaknesses in system operations, paying special attention to financial systems.

To expand on this important topic, the following discusses the exact functions of the internal EDP auditor, and what specific expertise he has to have to fulfill his responsibility.

5.1 THE EDP AUDITOR'S ROLE

For an internal EDP auditor (EDPA) to be effecitve, he must participate as a *consultant* in systems development from the Feasibility Study through the design and implementation. More precisely, to avoid the EDPA becoming subjective or complacent about any system he helped to create, he is *not* involved in the actual development cycle. He acts as a consultant to ensure that there are sufficient controls and effective audit trails in the design of new systems. He is, however, involved in the preparation of Risk Analysis, Contingency and Disaster Planning, as well as the testing of the Disaster Recovery Procedures.

Insofar as existing systems are concerned, the internal EDPA—in addition to non-EDP financial audits—checks and verifies software controls, identifies possible errors and vulnerable areas insofar as computer security is concerned, and reports his findings to management.

To perform his job the EDPA has to interview both professional and nonprofessional DP staff, examine documentation, follow the flow of data in a system by using the source code, do statistical sampling, automatic data test and validation, and verify that information in certain records is complete and accurate. Only a few years ago the EDPA could not perform the more sophisticated of the above tasks. He had to audit *"around the computer system,"* which included methods such as flowcharting by hand and then comparing it to the programmer's flowchart, and comparing line by line the production system against the documented system that management approved because he didn't have efficient software tools. But now he can audit *"through the computer system"* by using one of the many excellent audit software packages. Such specially designed audit programs allow the EDPA to access and test particular segments in data bases and records in master files *without* modifying or updating, that is, *without* causing any damage to any module or segment.

Obviously, the EDPA cannot possibly accomplish the above tasks unless his expertise includes data processing in addition to accounting. Moreover, because of the dynamic nature of the electronics field, it's essential that the EDPA keeps up with state-of-the-art high technology and computer security. He also has to have good communications skills and the ability to get along with management, systems analysts/designers, programmers, and users. Not an easy-to-fill job description. Perhaps that is the reason for the great demand for qualified EDP auditors.

5.2 SYSTEMS CONTROLS

Next in the prevention of software computer crime is systems controls. It is comprised of the following or similar measures:

5.2.1 Software Protection Level

As stated in Chapter 2, top management, basing their evaluation on risk assessment and cost/benefit analysis, must make the decision of *what software is to be protected* and *at what security level.* Such decision is necessary not only to comply with the Foreign Corrupt Practices Act and the Privacy Act (see Chapter 1), but also to achieve relative maximum data processing security. In addition, it is recommended that proprietary in-house developed sytems, applications, or programs be protected by trade secret status and/or copyright under the Computer Software Act of 1980. (For further information on this subject an attorney specializing in computer software protection should be consulted.)

5.2.2 Corporate Security Policy and Control Procedures

To deter computer crime and prevent the theft or abuse of company resources, a lucid corporate computer security policy and control procedures is to be published, distributed to the staff, and *rigorously enforced.* For example, each DP employee must have a clear understanding that unauthorized use of the company's computer systems and programs for playing games "just for the fun of it," or for private business such as making up the income tax for himself and friends, and/or running invoices for his brother-in-law's auto service shop, and the like, are explicitly *prohibited.*

A well written Security Policy and Control Procedures manual should make it crystal clear that first-time offenders will be reprimanded; that second-time offenders will be put on probation; and that third-time offenders will be terminated. Of course, any DP staff or user found altering (adding, deleting, or changing) any records, files, or programs for the purpose of fraud or embezzlement are to be reported immediately to the police and the FBI.

5.2.3 Software Protection Systems

Among the many excellent software security packages on the market are *ACF 2,* developed by SKK, Inc., and marketed by Cambridge Systems Group, *Top Secret,* developed by CGA Software Products Group, Inc., *Resource Access Control Facility (RACF),* developed by IBM, and *Access Control,* developed by Electronic Data Systems Group; one of the most popular seems to be the IBM product.

RACF* protects and monitors computer systems via the following features: It provides access control by a) identifying and verifying system users when they log on; b) allowing access to system resources only to users who are authorized to do so. Secondly, RACF monitors the system environment by logging detected unauthorized *attempts* as well as detected *actual accesses* to sensitive data or information in the system, and alerting proper personnel to such access violations via security reports. Simply put, RACF limits access to a DP facility's protected software resources by controlling: a) which staff may use the system; b) which parts of the system each user may access; and c) which components within those parts each user—according to his level of authorization—may access and how.

RACF performs its major functions by building "profiles" as to *who* is allowed to use *what* and *how* at the DP

*Copyright, IBM Corporation, Poughkeepsie, NY

facility—based on information input into RACF at the time it is implemented. These profiles—which reside on the RACF data set—contain descriptions of each user (who), each resource within the system (what), and the attributes and level of authorizations (how), as given to RACF by DP management. RACF uses these profiles to perform its user identification and authentication, and authorization checking and logging. See Figure 7 for an overview of the RACF environment.

Then there is also Michael Blank's *Intruder Detection System* (IDS). Unlike RACF and other access control software systems, IDS will accept any password. However, if the password is invalid, a message alerts the security officer to a security violation. Moreover, it identifies the terminal from which the invalid password is entered.

The unique part of this software system is that via its On-Line IDS subsystem it goes along with the intruder, as if the password was valid, thus ascertaining the intruder's intent, and providing the organization the necessary evidence to be able to prosecute the intruder. While its other subsystem, Batch IDS, collects all information relating to password errors, transaction errors, and files and records the intruder is trying to access. Batch IDS produces two reports: the Security Violations Report, which summarizes the events, and the Security Incident Report, which gives full details of each event. (See Figure 8 for an overview of IDS.)

The main thrust of IDS is deterring potential computer criminals from penetrating the company's computer system because of the threat of prosecution.

5.2.4 Systems and Programming Standards

If for no other reason, establishing systems and programming standards is essential for systems control. By defining,

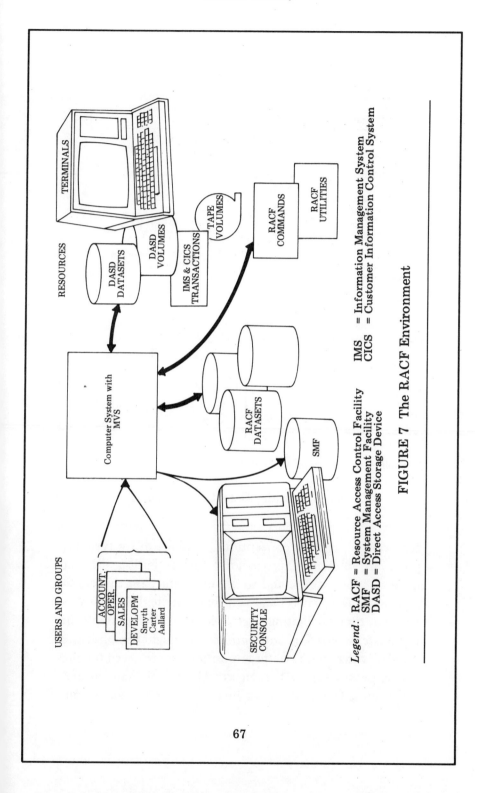

FIGURE 7 The RACF Environment

Legend: RACF = Resource Access Control Facility   IMS = Information Management System
           SMF = System Management Facility   CICS = Customer Information Control System
           DASD = Direct Access Storage Device

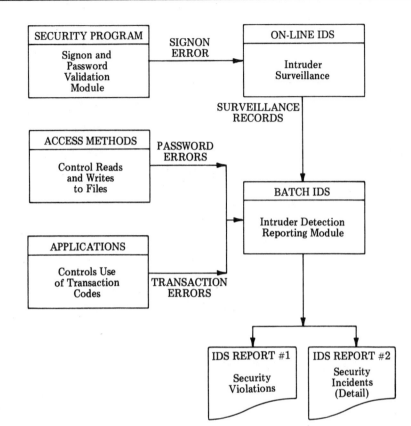

Through the courtesy of Michael Blank

FIGURE 8 Intruder Detection System (IDS)

for example, naming conventions or standards for systems, programs, job names, procedures, data definition, data set names, report names, and so on, uniformity for the length and meaning of such names throughout the DP facility is ensured, thus facilitating overall controls. For example, in the *Systems Naming Conventions* one might establish the standards that the first three positions are reserved for the particular system's ID, such as "MED" for Material and Engineering Data, "INC" for Inventory Control, and so on.

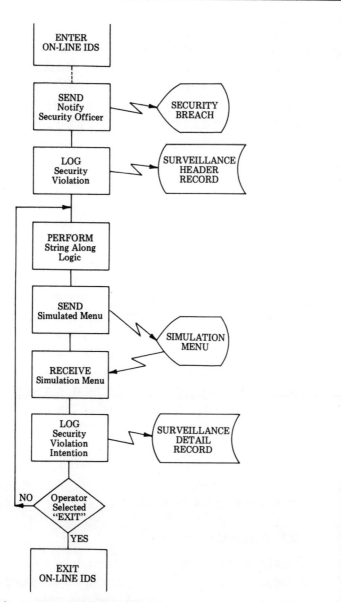

Through the courtesy of Michael Blank

FIGURE 9 On-Line IDS—Intruder Surveillance Sub-System

While in the *Program Naming Conventions* one might establish the standards that one position is reserved to show the type of program being used, such as "U" for update, "E" for edit, "S" for sort, "R" for restore, and so on, or that in coding "1" is used for Male, "2" is used for Female, and "3" is used for Unknown.

5.2.5 Password Security

For organizations that do not have one of the commercial software protection systems, an encoded password is the first line of defense against unauthorized access, especially in on-line systems. Passwords for access authorization levels are to be allocated on a "need to know" basis. They can be kept in the computer system—preferably in the data dictionary/ directory subsystem in a password file. The password file can be one-way encrypted, and it can allow the user to change his/her own password anytime. Better yet, the computer system can create the password at random, change it at a predetermined interval, and send it in a sealed envelope or through secured electronic mail to the appropriate user.

When a user enters his/her password and user ID, they are to be verified by the control file not only as to the ID but to the degree of eligibility (authorization level to selected data items, record types, and record type interrelations) before allowing access to any data.

5.2.6 Access Control Log

In addition to terminal lock and key, or magnetically encoded card inserted into the terminal (as discussed in Chapter 3) and a coded password, the computer system is to have an Access Control Log. The log identifies the number and location of the terminal being used, the date and time of the transaction, the file(s), record(s), and program(s) the person is accessing, as well as the ID and password of the user. This can serve as a record of transactions and a backup for the password verification process.

5.2.7 Systems Documentation

For systems control, as well as an essential reference for the EDP auditor and the DP staff, especially in case of sabotage or natural disaster, the documentation of all production systems are to be regularly updated, and kept in a fireproof safe. Moreover, the updated sections are to be recorded on the front page of the systems documentation manual and inserted at the proper sections. This is an important function, and a trusted staff should be given this responsibility.

5.3 APPLICATIONS CONTROLS

Applications controls designed into individual programs is another critical software crime deterrence measure. Typical applications controls include: input controls, processing controls, change controls, testing controls, and output controls.

5.3.1 Input Controls

Proper input controls insure that each transaction is processed correctly and only once, and that only authorized transactions enter the computer system. Input controls consist of the following:

a. *Batch totals* ensure in batch or sequential processing that the counted and totaled number and value of similar data items in an input batch are the same before and after processing. Normally, batch totals are prepared for each batch manually, which then are routed to data entry operator(s). Batch totals enable the system to compare and verify the computer totals against the batch totals.

Batch totals are also useful in an online environment. In an online system a flag is set on each record in the master file as it is accessed for processing. When the transaction enters the system, it doesn't actually update the master file immediately, instead it enters a transaction file. When sufficient transactions have been put into the transaction file, the actual documents are made into a batch, and updating the master records is done in a batch mode. In case of immediate updating, a batch can be prepared at the end of the day and checked against a computer generated transaction report.

b. *Hash totals* ensure that no items are lost or changed invalidly before or during processing by checking randomly selected fields for meaningless totals, such as the total of invoice serial numbers, the total of payroll or accounts payable checks serial numbers, and the like. Hash totals are excellent control tools.

c. *Record counts* ensure that all input records are processed. Because by themselves they do not prevent the dropping of a record followed by duplicate processing of an existing record or insertion of a new, unauthorized record; they are used as a mandatory addition to batch totals.

d. *Proper authorization* ensures that only data with proper authorization is entered into the system. In a batch-oriented system, proper authorization of records is usually done manually, prior to input. In addition, however, a password is usually required by the program, prior to the acceptance of the data by the system.

Because of on-line systems' capability for direct access to data files, on-line systems have to have more stringent authorization requirements than the batch-oriented system. Consequently, besides a password required to log on to the system, another level of password is usually necessary before transactions are accepted for input.

e. *Duplicate entry (key verification)* ensures accuracy of critical fields in a single record. By requiring that important data be entered twice in the same record, this control enhances the accuracy of processing.

f. *Data entry verification*—a very important control in batch-oriented systems. In this process, after one operator enters the data another data entry operator re-enters the same data. Next, either the data entry device or the computer system compares the re-entered data against the originally entered data and identifies any discrepencies between the two. Thus, the record can be corrected before it enters the system. Double checking the data entry may be somewhat costly, but it is an effective way to ensure that the data entering the system is accurate.

g. *Scheduling of processing* prevents the processing of unauthorized data. When data can only enter the system during specified intervals, it becomes quite difficult for an individual to prepare and process a batch of transactions without generating an output report that is distributed to people who monitor the system.

h. *Sequence checks of input documents* is another control to ensure that a particular transaction is entered into the system only once. If the input documents are prenumbered (purchase orders, for example), then these numbers are entered into the system only once. Otherwise, it is a relatively simple matter to have the computer store the processed transaction numbers and prevent duplicate processing by rejecting transactions that the files show have already been processed.

i. *Edits of data fields* verify the type of data. Most input devices have the capability of pre-establishing the format of an input record—including the type of data that will be in each field. This control enhances accuracy of input data by preventing the entry of alphabetic data in a numeric field, or vice versa.

5.3.2 Processing Controls

Processing controls verify that the transactions entered into the system are processed against the proper files; that each component of each transaction is valid; and that any invalid transaction rejected by the system is re-entered correctly. Typical processing controls are the following:

a. *File checks by program* ensure that proper files are used in the processing. By reading labels of the files available for processing, and verifying that they are the correct files, this control ensures that any edits to be performed on the input data will be done using the most current files, and that the updating process will affect only the proper files.

b. *Edits of data fields against computer tables* ensure that the information edited on the record is within acceptable norms. By comparing information in the input record (usually containing a certain amount of identifying and account destination data) with the existing file or a table of valid values, this control increases the reliability of the data.

c. *Tests of range values* help prevent processing of invalid data. By establishing ranges of acceptable values for certain items in an input record (even when it is not possible to have a direct comparison with a file or table, such as in the edit process), this control minimizes the processing of invalid data.

d. *Comparison of transaction corrections to a file of rejected transactions* ensures completeness of processing. This is because, normally, edits of data fields against computer tables will reject a certain number of transactions. These rejected records are stored in a suspense file and removed only as they are corrected. (The only exception to this should be if it is a proven duplicate transaction.) By comparing corrected transactions against a file of rejected transactions, this control reduces the posibility of a rejected item not being corrected and not re-entered.

e. *Internal control totals* help to identify program errors. By maintaining internal control totals which are computed in a separate portion of the program than the normal processing (unless various but related totals match), an exception report is generated. Consequently, this control ensures that processing is performed correctly.

5.3.3 Change Controls

Establishing change controls is essential for maintaining standard procedures in system and program modifications, and for safeguarding the integrity of the systems. It also serves as an effective deterrent against the potential embezzler or a disgruntled employee bent on sabotaging the company's system(s).

In setting up change controls the first consideration is to set up a Change Control Charter, after which a Change Control Committee can be formed.

a. *The Change Control Charter* determines the standard procedures, which has to be followed by any and all DP staff who has anything to do with system and program modifications—whether in programming, testing, implementing, or operating. Such written standards can prevent a programmer (either innocently or maliciously) from making a change in a program *without* asking for authorization and *without* telling anybody about it. An action that can have far-reaching and sometimes disastrous results.

The Change Control Charter also mandates that any user (including management) who wants a system or a program changed has to follow the standard procedures for requesting that change. These procedures include filling out a preprinted (management approved) service request (see Figure 10, Program Modification Service Request), getting authorization for the request, and submitting it to the Change Control Committee. These written standards can prevent users from interrupting a busy programmer and demanding that he drop everything else to modify that certain program immediately.

b. *The Change Control Committee,* which usually consists of a representative from DP management, computer operations, and the various user departments in addition to the internal EDP auditor, has the following responsibilities:

- determining the feasibility and appropriateness of the proposed change.

- measuring the scope of the requested change.

- measuring the impact of the proposed change on other systems, department functions, and operations.

- planning the implementation, if the proposed change is approved unanimously.

- coordinating the implementation.

- satisfying budget and audit requirements.

- periodically reviewing and, if necessary, updating the set of codes on which the Change Controls are based, and the Change Control Procedures.

c. *Updating of change control procedures.* As with systems documentation, it is absolutely necessary to assign a responsible DP employee to insert into all copies of the Change Control Procedures manuals the updates issued by the Change Control Committee.

d. *Logging changes into files and programs.* One of the responsibilities of the chief programmer or project manager is to check that the programmer who was given the task to perform a particular program modification, also logs the changes into the affected files and programs.

5.3.4 Testing Controls

To ensure that reliance can be placed in the system BEFORE a system becomes operational, testing controls must be included in the Corporate Security Policy and Control Procedures manual. The testing controls may include:

a. *Stringent administrative and physical controls setup* to protect live/valid data during the test cycle.

b. *Internal controls* to protect the system against abuse or serious error during the test cycle.

c. *Limited test files* of raw (unprocessed) data, and limited test files of processed data for module and system testing setup.

d. *Recording/documenting* of all activities (input, processing, errors, output) during the test cycle.

5.3.5 Output Controls

Output controls authenticate the previous controls by repeating the functions of input and processing controls. Such repetitive activities help to insure that only authorized transactions are processed correctly.

Output controls include the following:

a. *Comparison of output reports* to input and processing control totals ensures accurate and complete processing.

PROGRAM MODIFICATION SERVICE REQUEST

Request No. _____ (1)

| Initiated By: (2) | Extension No: (3) | Date Requested: (4) | Date Needed: (5) | Authorized By: (6) |

Group:

Purpose: (7)

Description of Update/Change: (8)

Areas Affected By the Above: (9)

Program Updated/Changed (10)

□ COBOL   □ VSI-LINKLIB
□ FORTRAN   □ VSI-SVCLIB
□ RPG-II   □ VSI-NUCLEUS

Timetable (11)

□ Effective immediately-information only
□ Effective at Next Unscheduled IPL
□ IPL is Scheduled At _____

□ CA-SORT   □ VSI-PROCLIB
□ MARK IV   □ VSI-PARMLIB
□ VALU-LIB II   □ VSI-USERPROG
□ PL/I
□ Other _____

□ Change has been Tested:
□ Change has Not been Tested:
□ Change Source is Vendor:
□ Change Source is in-house

Type of IPL Required
□ None   □ Cold Start   □ Warm Start   ⑫
□ Change to Init Deck
□ Change to Operating Procedure
□ Backoff Procedure

Est. Man Hours: ⑬	Estimated Cost: ⑭	Est. Completion Date: ⑮	Est. Proc. Time: ⑯	Actual Man Hours: ⑰

IMPLEMENTATION SCHEDULE	Date	Time	Initials
Verified By System Support ⑱	⑲	⑳	㉑
Approved By Operations ㉒			
Installation Completed ㉓			
Change Backed Off ㉔			

FIGURE 10

79

Specifically, if the computer system reduces the originally input batch totals by the values of the rejected transactions, the result can be compared with the total of the amounts used to update the files, and the amount printed on the output reports.

b. *Rejected transactions.* Reports of transactions rejected by the system during batch total verification or edits of individual transactions provide the information necessary to support some of the processing controls in section 5.3.2. They consist of items rejected during the current processing cycle *plus* items in the suspense file which have not yet been corrected. These reports can point to areas which need attention, so that the error rates can be reduced.

c. *Output reports control.* This function is a high-priority control not only because it is important that reports containing sensitive data go to authorized users solely, but because it's unlikely that an unauthorized user would be able to generate a batch of data and get it processed without the activity being identified by an authorized user and a member of the control group.

d. *Random comparison* of output to input documents verifies that processing is occurring normally. With the other controls in place, this control can be looked upon as a final test of the computer operation.

5.4 DP CRIME METHODS, DETECTION AND COUNTERMEASURES, AND POTENTIAL PERPETRATORS

The text that follows lists a number of possible DP crime methods, effective detection and countermeasures, and potential perpetrators. Actual case histories underline the fact that the critical component in any type of computer-related crime is *the human factor.*

5.4.1 Data Manipulation

Changing or adding data prior to or during input of data into the computer system is perhaps the most common means of committing computer-related theft or fraud among insiders who, as stated before, pose infinitely more threat to DP security than outsiders. This is especially true in time-sharing systems environments where the systems are user-friendly, and consequently vulnerable to manipulation by any unscrupulous DP staff member or end-user.

Case in point: Janet Blair, an employee at the Social Security Administration (SSA), Baltimore, Maryland, was charged on May 27, 1980 with forty three counts of forgery, conspiracy, and issuing false U.S. Treasury checks in the amount of $102,000. Blair perpetrated the computer-aided embezzlement by entering the issuance of fraudulant checks into the computer via her mainframe-connected intelligent terminal. Then, to avoid detection, as soon as the computer printed the checks, she put in a command to erase the audit trail of the illegal transactions. The fraud was detected not by SSA's auditors but by a Philadelphia bank official who became suspicious of a large number of cashed SSA checks bearing the same Social Security Number but made out to different names (friends of Blair). Blair received a sentence of eight years in federal prison and a fine of $500.

Detection and Countermeasures: the best detection against this specific type of computer crime is an internal EDP auditor who can use an EDP Audit software package to scrutinize transactions and review audit trails that indicate additions, changes, and deletions made to data files before or during processing. While batch totals, whether in a batch or online environment, can be an effective countermeasure against adding or deleting transactions in the input process. In addition, hash totals and check digits are good controls against changing data not only during input and processing but output as well.

Potential Perpetrators: programmer/analysts, data entry operators, computer operators, and end-users.

5.4.2 Trojan Horse

The *Trojan Horse* is a method whereby unauthorized instructions are inserted surreptitiously into a production program. It might be done to achieve material gains; to sabotage the program and botch up the system; or to have some "fun." The last category is usually done to see if a few extra instructions can have any impact on the performance of a program. Whatever the reason, this computer crime effects a monetary loss to the organization.

Case in point: Barry Wyche, a computer operator, hired at the DP facility of the University of Maryland Hospital, Baltimore, Maryland, in November, 1980, was arrested at the end of January, 1981. He was charged with embezzling $40,000 by inserting false invoices into the hospital's accounts payable production programs. Wyche, caught *in flagrante delicto* by his alert supervisor, was subsequently indicted, convicted, and sentenced to serve five years in the Maryland Division of Correction.

After Wyche was arrested, the hospital officials were chagrined to learn that the man not only had a criminal record, but that he was on probation for an identical offense when he was hired by the hospital.

Detection and Countermeasures: the most effectual detectin of such covert activities is still the human factor—an alert and responsible person working with the culprit. Insofar as countermeasures go, a review and tightening of the internal controls of the financial systems will do just fine. Also, as discussed in detail in the next chapter on Personnel Security, to prevent a person like Wyche from being hired for a sensitive job such as computer operator, each DP applicant should have a background security screening.

If a program is suspected of containing unauthorized instructions, it is the EDP auditor's responsibility to compare it with the master or backup copy. If confirmed that the program has been tampered with, the EDP auditor gives the task of finding the culprit to the security officer, and of rewriting the program to the DP manager or the chief programmer.

Potential Perpetrators: systems programmers, programmer /analysts, computer operators, and users.

5.4.3 Time Bomb

The time bomb which is called "logic bomb" by some, is quite similar to the above in technique. That is, unauthorized instructions are inserted into a program. But whereas the Trojan horse method is usually used for material gains, the time bomb method perpetrators have only one goal: *Sabotage.* Specifically, the instructions are written so that they are triggered to be executed on a predefined specific date or condition, to erase certain records or files, or cause a system to crash.

Case in point: In the spring of 1981, Justin Davis (not his real name), a 26-year-old maintenance programmer at the U.S. Department of Defense in Washington, D.C., was quite unhappy about being bypassed for promotion. He blamed his supervisor for it. And the longer Davis brooded about what, in his mind, was an "injustice," the more the time bomb way of "getting even" appealed to him. Because Davis was maintaining various programs for the Personnel and Payroll databases, he had access to these two systems.

Subsequently, he wrote the programming specifications for a time bomb program to erase a specific area in the Payroll data base in two years. But then he decided that he couldn't wait that long to get his revenge, and so he shortened the time period to six months. Because a thorough testing of the program might have aroused the data base administrator's suspicion, Davis skipped that phase. But he was confident that his program would perform exactly as he designed it.

Having his revenge weapon ready, Davis started looking around--via a DP employment agency—for another job in another city, far from Washington, D.C. When the employment agency arranged for him to be interviewed by an oil company in Dallas, Texas, for a programmer/analyst job, Davis took an early vacation at the beginning of September, 1981, and flew down to Texas. He was interviewed by the oil company's personnel director and the MIS manager, and a short time later they offered him the job. Davis, of course, accepted the offer.

At the end of his vacation, Davis returned to his job in Washington, D.C. On his very first day at the office he used the lunch hour—when nobody was around—to load his on-line program into the Payroll data base. That afternoon, at 4:45, he handed his supervisor a written termination, effective immediately.

Six months to the day after Davis quit his job, when the employees' monthly checks were scheduled to be processed, the payroll records of the ex-DP staff's whole department were erased. It took the data base administrator and a couple of systems programmers a lot of effort and much time to figure out what happened and to rebuild that particular section of the Payroll data base. The suspicion fell on Davis, but because they could not provide absolute proof to the authorities, the programmer could not be charged with the sabotage.

Detection and Countermeasures: the same as for the Trojan horse technique.

Potential Perpetrators: systems programmers, data base administrators, programmer/analysts.

5.4.4 Rounding Down or Salami Techniques

According to many EDP auditors rounding down is the simplest and safest way to steal via a computer system, especially if the perpetrator works for a large company. It involves reducing—either by a slight change in certain program(s), or by inserting extra instructions into a program(s) —the accounts of hundreds of saving or checking accounts by a couple of pennies, and transferring the amounts to an account under an assumed name. When the accumulated amount is large enough, the person can withdraw the money. The same method is used when calculating interests in financial accounts that result in fractions of the smallest denomination of money, yet which have to be rounded to the nearest cent. The programmer—if he has criminal tendencies—takes the fractions and deposits them in a fictitious account. Because the accounts are rounded to the nearest cent, the accounts are balanced, and the auditor, unless alerted by someone or something, is satisfied.

Detection and Countermeasures: in salami techniques, an audit of transactions will detect any anomaly. While the best countermeasures for this type of computer crime are random audit and analysis of several accounts by the EDP auditor, he may also want to compare the suspected program with the master or backup program.

Potential Perpetrators: programmer/analysts, systems programmers.

5.4.5 Scavenging

Scavenging is a method of obtaining data or information that may be left in or around a DP facility. Scavenging may be done physically or electronically.

    a. *Physical scavenging* involves searching of trash cans that are put outside the computer center to be picked up by the garbage collector. Such trash usually includes discarded interoffice memos, computer listings, input and purchase forms, outdated policy and procedures manual pages, and the like.

    b. *Electronic scavenging* involves searching for residual data left in a computer after the execution of a job.

Case in point: In December, 1970, Jerry Neal Schneider, a bright 21-year-old, posing as a freelance writer for national magazines, interviewed the public relations director of Pacific Telephone and Telegraph Company in Los Angeles, California—an organization Schneider was quite familiar with.

    In particular, this part-time electrical engineering student at Santa Monica College and discount telecommunications equipment vendor, knew all about the DP operations of the telephone company because, since his senior year at

Hamilton High School, Los Angeles, he had been scavenging the trash cans in front of the company's computer facility every morning.

Schneider convinced the public relations director, as well as the company's other executives, that an article by him about their sophisticated computerized equipment-ordering system in a national magazine would enforce the progressive image of the company. Consequently, they assigned a DP staff to Schneider to acquaint him with their operations.

For the next six months, while Schneider was ostensibly gathering material about the company and its sophisticated operations for an "authoritative" magazine article, he actually was updating his knowledge about their ordering procedures, and systematically developing a plan for a failsafe method to steal their equipment. An important part of his scheme included buying a 1962 Ford van at the annual telephone company auction, with the company's emblems still quite visible on the panels. A final touch was buying a gate key for $50 from a recently fired telephone company employee.

On June 21, 1971 Schneider—knowing the exact procedures of the telephone company's ordering system—started carrying out his scheme. He ordered telephones and switchboards in the amount of $30,000, to be delivered to one of the company's equipment sites that Schneider selected. According to the company's established schedule, the order was processed during the day, and the equipment delivered after midnight.

At dawn, before the telephone company employees started their workday, Schneider drove to the particular site in the old van he had bought at the auction; opened the gate with his key; loaded the van with the equipment he had ordered; took the bill of lading; drove out of the equipment site, and locked the gate behind him. He did not forget to sign the bill of lading with the name of one of the employees (who he had befriended) at that particular site, and then sent it in to the office.

Subsequently, he unloaded the equipment in a rented warehouse, and later sold the devices to unsuspecting customers.

Schneider, a confident young man, actually advertised in many trade journals that he could supply the latest, most sophisticated telecommunications equipment at bargain prices. But he was also a shrewd businessman. He did not keep a large inventory. In fact, he didn't steal any equipment until he received a prepaid order for it, and he didn't hire help until he absolutely needed it. Still, for the rest of the year, he ordered devices through the telephone company's ordering system almost every day, and then either he or a certain employee (who he trusted and rewarded generously) picked up the equipment in the old van at various sites.

Schneider felt safe. He checked and ascertained that as long as he ordered equipment within each supply site's budget, the telephone company purchasing department did not bother to verify each order.

In December, 1971, however, the "trusted" employee demanded more money for the early morning "pickups." Instead of giving in to the man, Schneider fired him. In turn, the employee, hoping for a large reward, told the telephone company about Schneider's operations. The company was incredulous, nevertheless they assigned two investigators to check out the young man's story.

Within less than a month the investigators verified the former employee's account of Schneider's method of stealing telephone company equipment. This, in turn, resulted in the District Attorney filing charges against Schneider.

At the end of February, 1972, Schneider was indicted on two charges of grand theft, two charges of burglary, and one charge of receiving stolen goods. On July 5, 1972, the Honorable Superior Court Judge, George M. Dell, sentenced Schneider to two months in a correctional institute, $500 fine, and a three-year probation.

Detection and Countermeasures: there are no known detection methods, only some efficacious countermeasures for scavenging. These countermeasures consist of shredding the discarded computer printouts and forms of all kinds, and checking the operating system to ensure that no residual data is left in the computer after execution of a job.

Potential Perpetrators: janitors, ground keepers, outsiders. In short, just about anybody can be a potential perpetrator of physical scavenging; while any DP professional or even a user can be a potential perpetrator of electronic scavenging.

5.4.6 Piggybacking

Piggybacking is a frequent method for gaining access to controlled access areas or for gaining access to sensitive information in the computer system. Piggybacking may be done physically or electronically.

---

a. *Physical piggybacking* may consist of the following scenario: an authorized employee opens the door to the computer room or the wire transfer room with his magnetic-strip card, and another employee—standing right behind him—goes in with him, even though he is not authorized to be in that room. Thus, it is possible for the piggybacking employee to do some damage to the DP operations, or to pick up a secret code or data to be used later in some fraud or embezzlement.

b. *Electronic piggybacking* usually happens in the following manner: a DP staff or a user sits down at an activated online intelligent terminal or desktop computer that an authorized programmer or user has forgotten to log off, or has just left for a few minutes. If the authorized person has a high authorization level, while the second person has low authorization level, the latter can access highly sensitive information that, if sold to a competitor, for example, could endanger the whole company.

Detection and Countermeasures: while as yet no known detection methods exist against piggybacking, positive countermeasures can be effected by educating the employees on the danger of piggybacking, and enforcing disciplinary actions if anybody is caught doing this sort of computer abuse.

Potential Perpetrators: any and all employees who, on account of limited authorization level, can only retrieve and review nonconfidential data on their video display terminals.

5.4.7 Unauthorized Accessing

Unauthorized accessing is perhaps the most publicized computer crime method. An unusual aspect of this technique is that—at least so far—it is perpetrated by young people. These "hackers" or "electronic invaders," as the unauthorized accessing students are called, up until recently broke into the computer systems of government and private institutions and companies because it was a "challenge." But now, at least in one case, a student broke into a computer system for profit.

Unauthorized accessing is usually done through a personal computer that (with a modem) has telecommunications capability. The hackers, working tirelessly for hours and hours, try every possible combination to get particular access codes. When one of them gets through to some government agency or company's computer system, he publishes that access code on the electronic network bulletin boards that computer buffs have access to. Thus, the hackers accumulate many access codes which they use for their enjoyment, regardless of how much damage they may do.

Detection and Countermeasures: presently, the best detection method against hackers is the Intruder Detection System (see 5.2.3). As to countermeasures: the growing number of strict laws regulating such and similar practices are most effective. The fact is that twenty-three states (including California as of January 1, 1984) have adopted legislation making it a crime to tamper with or steal from computer systems (see Chapter 1).

Potential Perpetrators: anybody, but especially teenage students, who have a personal computer with telecommunications capability.

5.4.8 Computer Security Breach

A breach of security is more of a failure to observe the confidentiality of certain data or information that the person is processing, than it is a computer crime. Still, it is included here because it can do a lot of damage.

Case in point: Stan Leskin, a data entry operator, employed in 1983 by Yourdon, the New York based DP Management

91

Consulting Company, breached the company's Unix system which held sensitive information, such as the salaries of the employees.

Leskin, working with these files, saw the figures, and proceeded to tell some of his coworkers that they were not earning as much as others in their particular department.

When a group of employees started to complain to their managers about the inequity in salaries, the managers got together. At the meeting they agreed that there was a good possibility that the Unix system was breached. The trouble was, however, that they had no idea who the guilty party might have been. Consequently, they laid a trap for the culprit by entering fictitious information into the system about an imminent major corporate reorganization.

The data entry operator accessed the "confidential information," and immediately began spreading the news about the corporate "shake-up." Leskin was so obvious that there was no question as to who was doing the computer security breach, and he was immediately fired.

Detection and Countermeasures: the above methods for the detection and countermeasures against disclosing confidential or proprietary information are as good as any.

Potential Perpetrators: programmer/analysts, data entry operators, computer operators, and users.

6

Personnel Security

SIX
Personnel Security

Given that people and human factors are synonymous, a strong, constructive personnel management philosophy can provide a powerful deterrence against computer crime.

Now, sophisticated physical, hardware, and software monitoring systems, security guards, effective systems and applications controls, encryption, and internal and external EDP auditors make it more difficult for a potential computer criminal to steal or copy software and data, embezzle, sell confidential information, steal CPU time, use programs and applications covertly for private projects, or carry out a vendetta and sabotage the system.

But it is not enough! Unless there is a definitive and enforceable personnel security policy—based on a positive management philosophy covering rules of conduct and employment life cycle from hiring, continued education, performance evaluation, promotion, mandatory annual two weeks vacation to termination—no maximum or even relative DP security can be achieved.

Besides, a realistic appraisal of the security risks inherent in any DP environment is not complete unless it includes personnel security risks. These risks must take into consideration every DP employee, from data entry operator to programmer/analyst, to DP manager and MIS director. In other words, every DP staff's background must be screened thoroughly.

6.1 BACKGROUND INVESTIGATION

Granted that *good* human resources in the DP fields are not easy to obtain, nevertheless establishing specific procedures for recruiting and hiring—which include conducting background security checks—is essential. Moreover, these procedures are to be observed *without exception,* even when the applicant is a highly valued DP professional such as a DP manager, MIS director, DBMS (data base management systems) administrator, systems programmer, telecommunications analyst, or computer operations manager.

Case in point: two DP professionals—Eugene B. Slear, an assistant director, and one of his staff, Thomas M. Boyle, a programmer/analyst—who worked at the DP facility of the University of Maryland Hospital in Baltimore, were indicted in 1982 for computer-assisted embezzlement.

Slear, a handsome, well-dressed man with a taste for high living, was hired by the University of Maryland Hospital as assistant director for DP finance and computer systems in January, 1979. His accounting background *and* DP experience plus excellent professional references from his last two positions that covered five years made him a well-qualified applicant. He impressed all the people who interviewed him with his "professional attitude." And the university officials congratulated themselves for hiring such a "good man."

Had there been a total personnel security policy in place, the hospital management could have avoided a financial loss and bad publicity. Point in fact: if the hospital would have conducted a security check* on the likeable and knowledgeable Slear, they would have found that in 1973, he served a sentence in the Baltimore County jail for embezzlement from a large company where he worked as a bookkeeper.

After serving his term, he used his familiarity with accounting and electronic data processing (which, according to certain sources he learned in jail) to secure a job at a computer center. His rise was remarkable. This was partly due to his knowledge, but mostly because he had the ingredients of a successful executive. He knew how to communicate with management *and* be on good terms with his peers and subordinates. Slear also had a great sense of timing for leaving one company for another, more prestigious job at a higher salary.

Less than a month after he started in his new job at the University of Maryland Hospital, Slear hired Thomas M.

---

*While the personnel manager (or anybody for that matter) cannot write or call a District Attorney's office to check if a job applicant has or has not a criminal record, he can—according to the Public Information Act—write any city's Criminal Records Clerk's Office in any of the fifty states for particulars about an individual. (For possible exception see Chapter 1, section 4.) In fact, any person can go into such an office—including indicted and convicted criminals —and request the "rap sheet" or the trial transcriptions of anybody, including his own, and read them, but *not* take them out of the office.

An example is Ross Eugene Fields, aka (also known as) Harold J. Smith, aka Harold Rossfields Smith, the highly publicized flamboyant sports promoter. During his 37-day trial in the latter part of 1981 for embezzling $21.3 million from Wells Fargo Bank in Los Angeles (between August, 1978 and January, 1981), Fields visited almost daily the Office of the Clerk, of the U.S. District Court for the Central District of California. He pored over the transcripts of his previous day's trial and made copious notes to provide his lawyer, Howard Moore, Jr., with material beneficial for his defense. Fields, by the way, was convicted in January, 1982 and sentenced for ten years in a federal prison. He was also fined $30,000. (More on Fields, the acknowledged "pro of computer crime," in section 6.2.)

Boyle, Jr., a programmer/analyst to help design, develop, and implement a new, badly needed accounts receivable and billing systems for the hospital.

Early in February, 1980, Slear *allegedly* took Boyle to lunch in an expensive restaurant. During lunch Slear took Boyle into his confidence and disclosed that he was in a bad financial situation, but that he knew a way whereby both he *and* his subordinate could get lots of money.

When Boyle showed signs of interest, Slear revealed his "fail-safe blueprint." The scheme consisted of Boyle entering fictitious invoices typed on fictitous software firms' letterheads into the hospital's Accounts Payable system. And, as Slear was quick to point out, since he, as assistant director of DP finance and systems, approved all payments for DP-related bills, there was little danger that management would discover the embezzlement.

At first Boyle was rather reluctant, but he needed his recently acquired job. Besides, Slear was a very persuasive superior.

Subsequently, according to the indictment, Boyle set up fictitious accounts in the hospital's Accounts Payable system, and from February, 1980, to March, 1981, they embezzled $126,564. In addition, Slear accepted $41,095 in cash and merchandise as "gratuities" from a vendor to whom he awarded a $60,00 software contract.

However, by the end of March, 1981, Slear's "persuasion" notwithstanding, Boyle refused to go on with the scam.

Many months before Boyle's refusal, to be precise in October, 1980, management informed Slear that their external auditing firm, Coopers & Lybrand, were scheduled to do their year-end auditing of the hospital's DP operations. Quick-thinking Slear, stating that he needed more time to have the newly implemented systems running smoothly and without any errors, asked his superiors to put off the auditing for a while. The officials agreed, and Slear—for over seven months—was successful in postponing the auditing.

In May, 1981, increasingly pressured by the hospital's top management to have the auditors conduct a security audit, Slear responded to a newspaper ad from a steel company in Pennsylvania. The company was looking for a vice-president for their data processing facility. When Slear appeared for the interview, the steel company management liked what they saw. They made him an attractive offer, and Slear accepted it. On June 1, 1981—just days before the overdue EDP auditing began—he resigned from his position at the University of Maryland Hospital, and went to work for the steel company in Pennsylvania.

The $126,564 embezzlement and the $41,095 bribery came to light in late June, 1981, when Coopers & Lybrand were able to audit the DP operations. In July, 1981, both Slear and Boyle were arrested and later released on bail. Slear was found guilty on December 7, 1983, and sentenced on bribery charges to an eighteen-month prison term in the Department of Corrections; while Boyle, who pleaded guilty on November 4, 1982, was sentenced on October 4, 1983, to an eighteen-month prison term (with eight months suspended for time already served) to be followed by five years of supervised probation.

As is usually the case, after this "incident," the hospital belatedly instituted background security checks for all of its DP personnel, and tightened the internal controls in its financial systems.

6.2 CAREER-PATHING

Now, a security investigation that includes contacting the applicant's work references, checking the applicant's background with the proper authorities, and verifying the applicant's school references will eliminate DP staff with criminal records and phony degrees. However, unless there is an affirmative personnel follow-up system ensuring that employees' performances and skills are routinely reviewed, updated via some type of performance evaluation system, and considered in a well-structured career-pathing, the probability that an employee (without any prior criminal record) becomes disgruntled and turns to some form of computer crime is always present.

Furthermore, an effective follow-up system can prevent job frustration if not job stress. It can maintain high employee morale by ensuring that knowledgeable, productive personnel are not languishing in some tedious, low-level jobs and tasks but are given opportunities for more challenging, better paying positions.

Case in point: Lloyd Benjamin Lewis, the assistant operations officer at the Beverly Hills branch of Wells Fargo Bank, who became quite discontent with lack of promotions, and consequently was susceptible to the previously mentioned Ross Eugene Fields' seductive proposition about a "fail-safe" embezzlement.

Fields's computer-related bank fraud scheme, which involved Lewis, was based on a "roll-over" method devised by Sammie Marshall (another disgruntled bank employee, and a friend of Fields) and perfected by the funds-hungry sport promoter.

The ingenious "roll-over" scam that bypassed the bank's internal computer accounting system and thus tapped into the bank's rich interbranch settlement funds went something like this:

Whenever Fields wrote out a check or whenever a cashier's check was issued for him by Lewis in amounts anywhere from $19,007.50 to $250,000, the assistant operations officer offset the debit with false credit by misencoding (with the secret code stolen by Marshall from another Los Angeles branch of the bank) the two-part interbranch settlement form before entering the transaction into the computer. Thus, the bank's computer system, which was designed to check the credit transactions from each *issuing branch* and the corresponding debit transactions from each *receiving branch* before processing the daily transactions, was "fooled." That is, with the debits and credits seemingly balanced, the bank's interbranch computer system accepted Lewis's transactions for processing.

Subsequently, Lewis—between September, 1978, and January 14, 1981—funneled some $21.3 million out of the bank, with most of the money going into the hands of his mentor, Fields.

Lewis was able to continue with this grand-scale embezzlement by never being late or absent from work, and by not taking a vacation for over two years—something that went *unnoticed* by his superiors.

Then on January 14, 1981, something happened, and the scheme that worked so well for over two years came to an abrupt end.

To this day Lewis doesn't know just exactly what he did "wrong." But the fact of the matter was that the bank's computer system detected an anomaly in the interbranch settlement funds, and red-flagged Lewis's transactions. The transactions were examined carefully, and on January 23, 1981, Lewis's supervisor and the branch manager confronted the assistant operations officer with "unassailable proof" of his illegal activities. The man fled in panic.

However, after thinking it over, on February 3, 1981, the fugitive Lewis went to the nearest FBI office and turned himself in. On June 1, 1982, Lewis was convicted and sentenced to five years in federal prison.

6.3 POSSIBLE INDICATORS OF DISCONTENTMENT

Symptoms that just might indicate a disgruntled employee and symptoms that a DP manager will want to investigate expeditiously but in a low-key manner are:

- Excessive absenteeism *or* unwarranted overtime
- Persistent late arrival for work
- Sudden low-quality and low-production output
- Complaints
- Putting off vacation

Any or all of these symptoms may only indicate job frustration or job stress and not disgruntlement. However, a DP manager knows that such things are often the catalysts for computer crime, and will not ignore any such signs, but look into any possible problem by communicating with the particular person on a one-to-one basis in the privacy of his office.

By talking to the employee as soon as possible, the DP manager can minimize if not completely eliminate job frustration and consequent possible security threats.

6.4 PROPER SECURITY ORIENTATION FOR NEW DP EMPLOYEES

To impress upon new DP employees the importance of security relating to *every* phase of data processing, including the necessity of having *controlled access* to copying machines; to involve new DP employees in computer security measures and controls; and to make them feel that it is their responsibility to report (instead of looking the other way) any security violations, that's what proper security orientation is all about. And it *can be accomplished* by informative educational seminars given by knowledgeable security professionals who are also good communicators.

6.5 SEPARATION OF DUTIES OF DP STAFF

It is essential that separation of duties and responsibilities are established in a DP facility. Thus, employees who prepare source documents are not to enter data into the computer system and perform verification. Data entry operators in batch processing, for example, are to be divided into two groups: the first group to enter the data into the terminals, and the second group to verify that the input data is accurate *before* the data is processed.

Similarly, the applications programmer who codes, tests, and debugs programs in a new or modified system, is not to be the person who tests the completed programs in the Systems Tests. The reason is twofold: a) the programmer, being proud of his creation, consciously or unconsciously does not want to find anything wrong with his programs, and so he will overlook "inconsequential bugs." But "inconsequential bugs" have a way of becoming "big trouble" and cause systems to malfunction; b) the systems analyst, the EDP auditor, and the users can verify via the Systems Tests that the programs respond to their requirements. Finally, the DP employee whose duty is to reconcile batch totals, for example, is not to be the same person who either prepares the batch totals, or the person who inputs the data for processing from source documents.

As an aside, in the business world the person who signs the check is never the person who prepares it.

6.6 EFFECTIVE PERFORMANCE EVALUATION SYSTEMS

There are several excellent commercial job evaluation/job comparison point system packages available. One of the best known is the "Hay Guide Chart-Profile Method" or the "Hay System." It was developed by Hay Associates, an international management consulting firm headquartered in Philadelphia, Pennsylvania.

6.6.1 The Hay System

In simple terms, the Hay System—focusing on jobs and not on individuals—describes and evaluates qualifications that are important to any job at any level. The three primary components that this technique uses to evaluate jobs are: *know-how, problem solving,* and *accountability.*

Before starting on these measures, however, there is a preliminary step that is basic to the Hay System: acquiring a complete understanding of the particular job to be evaluated. This is effected via written job descriptions that are not merely lists of requirements. The job descriptions that are fundamental to the Hay System detail the functions, responsibility, authority, *and* the place of each job in the hierarchy of the organization.

In the final step, each job's "profile" (the total sum of know-how, problem solving, and accountability) is compared to another job's "profile" as it relates to the enterprise and the particular field or industry the company operates in.

A brief description of Hay System *through the courtesy of Hay Associates* follows.

The process in the Hay System begins with a small group of carefully selected benchmark job descriptions which represent the starting point. Evaluation of these jobs are based on multiple judgments about the relativity of the three components: 1) know-how, 2) problem solving, and 3) accountability. These elements make up each job, and are expressed on an evaluation scale of numbers. First the definitions:

---

1. *Know-how* is the sum total of every kind of skill acquired, and necessary for an acceptable job performance. It is the requirement for:

- Practical procedures, specialized techniques, and scientific disciplines.
- Integrating and harmonizing diversified functions involved in managerial situations that occur in operating, supporting, and administrative fields. This know-how may be exercised consultatively (about management) as well as executively, and involves in some combination the areas of organizing, planning, executing, controlling, and evaluating.
- Active, practicing, face-to-face skills in the area of human relationship.

Measuring Know-how: Know-how has both scope (variety) and depth (thoroughness). Thus, a job may require some knowledge about a lot of things, or a lot of knowledge about a few things. The total know-how is the combination of scope and depth: "How much knowledge about how many things."

2. *Problem solving* is the amount of original thinking required by the particular job for analyzing, evaluating, creating, reasoning, arriving at, and making conclusions and/or decisions to solve a specific problem.

Problem solving has two dimensions:

- The thinking environment in which problems are solved.
- The challenge presented by the problems to be solved.

3. *Accountability* is the answerability for actions and for the consequences of those actions. It is the measured effect of the job on end results.

Accountability has three dimensions:

- *Freedom to act:* The degree of personal or procedural control and guidance.
- *Job impact on end results:* The controlling impact on end results, where shared accountability of others is subordinate.
- *Magnitude:* indicated by the general dollar size of the area(s) most clearly or primarily affected by the job (on an annual basis).

The numbering system used universally in the Hay System is a geometric scale with a ratio of approximately 15 percent between terms in the series. That is, the value of each aspect grows in 15 percent increments.

Multiple judgement on the job aspects are gained from three sources.

---

1. *Management committee.* By using a group of qualified people to evaluate jobs, more than one person's judgment is brought to bear on the same subject.

2. *Ranking and rating.* This source is procedural in nature, and involves measurement of job content by several means such as ranking and rating. *Ranking* is self-explanatory; while *rating* means establishing not only a rank order, but also a number of intervals between jobs. In measuring job content, the lowest know-how position is arbitrarily assigned a number in the geometric series.

Having established this base, jobs with higher know-how have their step numbers (1, 2, 3, 4, and so on) converted appropriately to the other numbers in the geometric scale. For example, if 50 is chosen as the point value for the lowest know-how job in the benchmark sample, and the job with the next higher know-how is one step, the value of the know-how of that job would be 57—the next value in the geometric scale. Table 1 illustrates the relationship between the terms in the geometric scales and the step value.

3. *Profiling* is the third source in the job aspects that contributes to multiple judgments. In simple terms, a profile of a job is the proportion of know-how, problem solving, and accountability which make up the total job. Because it is a practical business judgment, it is often fairly easy to recognize a job as being primarily a know-how job (for example, data entry operator), or an accountability job (for example, MIS director or DP manager), or a heavy "think" job (for example, systems programmer, systems analyst). These statements are qualitative profiling judgments.

RELATIONSHIP BETWEEN GEOMETRIC
SCALE AND STEP VALUE

Geometric Scale	Step Value
50*	1
57	2
66	3
76	4
87	5
100	6
115	7
132	8
152	9
175	10

*The starting point for the scale is set arbitrarily. The scale can be started with any number in the series, since it is the ratio between the numbers that is important to the measurement, not their absolute value.

TABLE 1

When evaluators go a step further and attach relative numerical values to these statements, saying that a given job appears to consist of X percent know-how, Y percent problem solving, and Z percent accountability, all adding to 100 percent, they are making a perceptive and useful profiling judgment.

The Guide Charts (see Figures 11 through 14) are predesigned and used tentatively as a starting point. Jobs are evaluated by:

1. Gaining a thorough understanding of job content.

2. Slotting jobs on each grid.

3. Selecting an appropriate value in each cell on each grid. Ultimately, this determination rests upon direct comparison between the job under consideration and jobs that have been measured previously.

4. The point values for know-how, problem solving, and accountability for the job are added to get the total evaluation points. By calculating the percentages of the above factors—as expressed in these number statements—a profile develops which provides an independent check on the proper use of the Guide Charts.

5. After a number of jobs have been evaluated, for example, forty to fifty, the results of the whole group are reviewed for obvious inconsistencies. Where necessary, corrections are made. During this process the tentative Guide Charts themselves are tested for applicability to the given situation. Where indicated, appropriate adjustments are made to reflect facts about the jobs and the company.

109

KNOW-HOW

		Managerial Know-How											
		I. Minimal			II. Related			III. Diverse			IV. Broad		
		1.	2.	3.	1.	2.	3.	1.	2.	3.	1.	2.	3.
A. Primary	1	50	57	66	66	76	87	87	100	115	115	132	152
	2	57	66	76	76	87	100	100	115	132	132	152	175
	3	66	76	87	87	100	115	115	132	152	152	175	200
B. Elementary Vocational	1	66	76	87	87	100	115	115	132	152	152	175	200
	2	76	87	100	100	115	132	132	152	175	175	200	230
	3	87	100	115	115	132	152	152	175	200	200	230	264
C. Vocational	1	87	100	115	115	132	152	152	175	200	200	230	254
	2	100	115	132	132	152	175	175	200	230	230	264	304
	3	115	132	152	152	175	200	200	230	264	264	304	350
D. Advanced Vocational	1	115	132	(152)	152	175	200	200	230	264	264	304	350
	2	132	152	175	175	200	230	230	264	304	304	350	400
	3	152	175	200	200	230	264	264	304	350	350	400	460
E. Basic Technical-Specialized	1	152	175	200	200	230	264	264	304	350	350	400	460
	2	175	200	230	230	264	304	304	350	400	400	460	528
	3	200	230	264	264	304	350	350	400	460	460	528	608

F.	Seasoned Technical-Specialized	200 230 264	230 264 304	264 304 350	264 304 350	304 350 400	350 400 460	350 400 460	400 460 528	460 528 608	460 528 608	528 608 700	608 700 800	
G.	Technical-Specialized Mastery	264 **304** 350	304 350 400	350 400 460	350 400 460	400 460 528	460 528 608	460 528 608	528 608 700	608 **700** 800	608 700 800	700 800 920	800 900 1056	
H.	Professional Mastery	350 400 460	400 460 528	460 528 608	460 528 608	528 608 700	608 700 800	608 700 800	700 800 920	800 920 1056	800 920 1056	920 1056 1216	1056 1216 1400	
		TOTAL	AC	PS	KH	TOTAL	AC	PS	KH	PS	AC	TOTAL		

KH	PS	AC	TOTAL
152			

SUPERVISOR KEY PUNCH

KH	PS	AC	TOTAL
304			

ACTUARIAL SPECIALIST
RESEARCH ASSOCIATE

KH	PS	AC	TOTAL
700			

AREA MANAGER

FIGURE 11

Through the courtesy of Hay Associates

PROBLEM SOLVING

1 → **2** ↑

Thinking Challenge

Problem Solving	1. Repetitive		2. Patterned		3. Interpolative		4. Adaptive		5. Uncharted		
A. Strict Routine	10%	12%	14%	16%	19%	22%	25%	29%	33%	38%	A
B. Routine	12%	14%	16%	19%	22%	25%	29%	33%	38%	43%	B
C. Semi Routine	14%	16%	19%	22%	25%	29%	33%	38%	43%	50%	C
D. Standardized	16%	19%	22%	25%	29%	33%	38%	43%	50%	57%	D
E. Clearly Defined	19%	22%	25%	29%	33%	38%	43%	50%	57%	66%	E
F. Broadly Defined	22%	25%	29%	33%	38%	43%	50%	57%	66%	76%	F
G. Generally Defined	25%	29%	33%	38%	43%	50%	57%	66%	76%	87%	G
H. Abstractly Defined	29%	33%	38%	43%	50%	57%	66%	76%	87%	100%	H

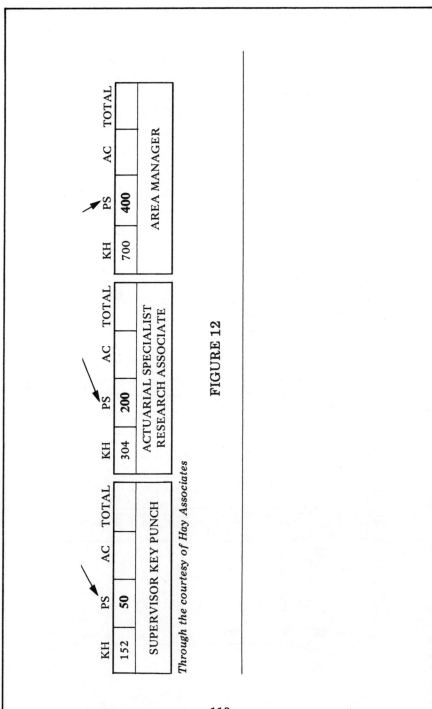

FIGURE 12

Through the courtesy of Hay Associates

ACCOUNTABILITY

1 → 2 ↑ 3 ↑

	(1) Very Small Or Indeterminate				(2) Small				(3) Medium				(4) Large		
	R	C	S	P	R	C	S	P	R	C	S	P	R	C
A. Prescribed	10	14	19	25	14	19	25	33	19	25	33	43	25	33
	12	16	22	29	16	22	29	38	22	29	38	50	29	38
	14	19	25	33	19	25	33	43	25	33	43	57	33	43
B. Controlled	16	22	29	38	22	29	38	50	29	38	50	66	38	50
	19	25	33	43	25	33	43	57	33	43	57	76	43	57
	22	29	38	50	29	38	50	66	38	50	66	87	50	66
C. Standardized	25	33	43	57	33	43	57	76	43	57	76	100	57	76
	29	38	50	(66)	38	50	66	87	50	66	87	115	66	87
	33	43	57	76	43	57	76	100	57	76	100	132	76	100
D. Generally Regulated	38	50	66	87	50	66	87	115	66	87	115	152	87	115
	43	57	76	100	57	76	100	132	76	(100)	132	175	100	132
	50	66	87	115	66	87	115	152	87	(115)	152	200	115	152
E. Directed	57	76	100	132	76	100	132	175	100	132	175	230	132	175
	66	87	115	152	87	115	152	200	115	152	200	264	152	200
	76	100	132	175	100	132	175	230	132	175	230	304	175	230

F. Oriented Direction															
87	115	152	200	115	152	200	264	152	200	264	350	200	264	350	264
100	132	175	230	132	175	230	304	175	230	304	400	230	304	400	304
115	152	200	264	152	200	264	350	200	264	350	460	264	350	460	450
G. Broad Guidance															
132	175	230	304	175	230	304	400	230	304	400	528	304	400	304	400
152	200	264	350	200	264	350	460	264	350	460	608	350	460	350	460
175	230	304	400	230	304	400	528	304	400	528	700	400	528	400	528
H. Strategic Guidance															
200	264	350	460	264	350	460	608	350	460	608	800	460	608	460	608
230	304	400	528	304	400	528	700	400	528	700	920	528	700	528	700
264	350	460	608	350	460	608	800	460	608	800	1056	608	800	608	800
I. Generally Unguided															
304	400	528	700	400	528	700	920	528	700	920	1216	700	920	700	920
350	460	608	800	460	608	800	1056	608	800	1056	1400	800	1056	800	1056
400	528	700	920	528	700	920	1216	700	920	1216	1600	920	1216	920	1216

KH	PS	AC	TOTAL
152	50	66	268

SUPERVISOR KEY PUNCH

KH	PS	AC	TOTAL
304	200	115	619

ACTUARIAL SPECIALIST RESEARCH ASSOCIATE

KH	PS	AC	TOTAL
700	400	608	1708

AREA MANAGER

FIGURE 13

Through the courtesy of Hay Associates

115

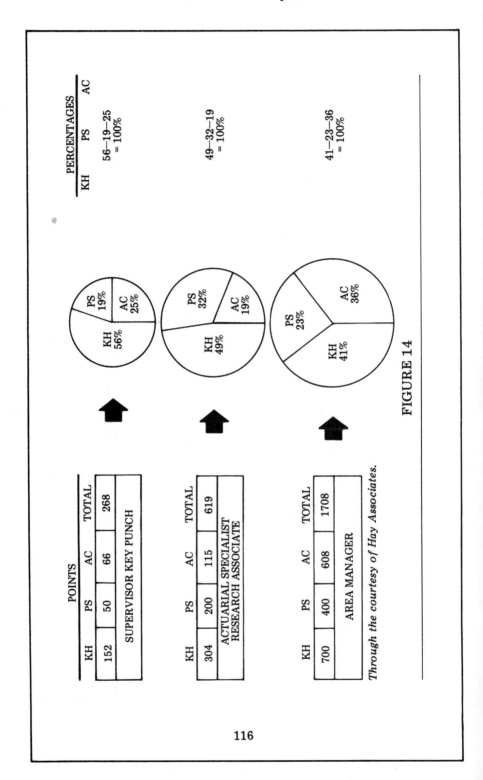

PERCENTAGES

KH	PS	AC
	56—19—25 = 100%	
	49—32—19 = 100%	
	41—23—36 = 100%	

PS 19% AC 25% KH 56%

PS 32% AC 19% KH 49%

PS 23% AC 36% KH 41%

POINTS

KH	PS	AC	TOTAL
152	50	66	268

SUPERVISOR KEY PUNCH

KH	PS	AC	TOTAL
304	200	115	619

ACTUARIAL SPECIALIST RESEARCH ASSOCIATE

KH	PS	AC	TOTAL
700	400	608	1708

AREA MANAGER

FIGURE 14

Through the courtesy of Hay Associates.

With the total points now available for a variety of jobs, a salary structure is established by plotting a *scattergram* of existing salaries on the vertical axis against point values on the horizontal axis. This leads ultimately to the establishment of a salary structure for the company with minimums, maximums, and midpoints.

6.7 ROTATING PERSONNEL DUTIES

An effective personnel security and follow-up system does more than just prevent qualified DPers to be forgotten in mediocre jobs. It also defines policies and procedures for a whole range of activities such as: a) rotating personnel duties, such as work assignments for programmers, work schedules for computer operators, and so on; b) requiring two people to be present in the machine room at all times; c) not allowing computer operators to make changes in programs, or override errors on the console; d) not allowing programmers to come into the machine room and operate the computer, not even with an operator present; e) enforcing mandatory annual two weeks vacation for all DP staff; f) communicating to every DP staff at every level that discussion of sensitive information (trade secrets, password, and the like) outside the facility could be ground for reprimand or even dismissal; g) following strict procedures for terminations, especially when an employee is fired.

The last two procedures usually include handing a severance check to the terminated staff and physically escorting the person out of the building. Moreover, to ensure that the fired employee does not have the opportunity to sabotage data files, equipment, or whatever, the security guards are given instructions *never* to allow that person back into the facility. Even when an employee resigns, the person is usually given a two-week or a month severance pay, and asked to pack and leave the facility immediately. It's a bad personnel security policy that allows a former DP employee to "hang around."

6.8 THE BUDGET CONTROL ISSUE IN DP SECURITY

The impact of cutting or "bringing the DP department budget under control" on the staff must be considered as a possible personnel security threat. Consequently, it behooves the DP manager to convince his staff that controlling the budget is in the best interest of everybody. He also has to be able to assure all DP employees that if any tasks have to eliminated, the person(s) affected will be transferred to another department (if possible), or retrained for another job. The primary thrust here is to involve the personnel and get their cooperation in a painful but usually very necessary procedure, so that the price of a controlled budget is not disgruntled employees.

6.8.1 Organizational Modeling

There are many ways to bring about budget control. One method that seems to gain popularity is the *organizational modeling*. This technique is used to *identify* marginal areas of activity (costs disproportionate to their value), and *determine* the method to reduce their costs, or completely eliminate them.

Organizational modeling technique consists of the following steps:

---

1. A model of the department is constructed. The model includes all the staff, the tasks they perform, the material (input, source documents, and so on) and hardware they use in performing the tasks.

2. The work of the department is defined insofar as the input and its usage in tasks, and it is determined how much each task costs in terms everybody can understand—dollars. The same calculation is applied to underutilized hardware. Thus, each measurable task's cost is analyzed as it relates to the cost of end products or services the MIS/DP department provides to the inhouse or outside users.

3. A detailed report based on the cost of each activity is generated. It contains specific recommendations for better utilization of personnel, time, material, and equipment, for reducing if not eliminating unproductive tasks, and for increasing productivity and benefit to the department (and the company as a whole) through Quality Assurance.

6.8.2 Overhead Value Analysis

Another method that is specifically designed to control overhead/budget is McKinsey & Company's *Overhead Value Analysis (OVA)*. The following description of this widely used technique is presented through the courtesy of McKinsey & Company, Inc., New York.

In the OVA process the emphasis is on eliminating or reducing unnecessary *work*. The intent is *not* to get people to work harder, but simply to find ways of reducing unnecessary work output. Roughly two-thirds of all savings in an average OVA program comes from reduction of output.

Thus, the difference in the OVA process is that *managers* value the end products and services they produce or request in relation to the cost of producing them. First, every end product of a department is listed together with the activities required to produce it. Then each end product and activity is scrutinized to see whether it can be eliminated, reduced, or streamlined.

Potential cost savings are weighed against the risks of elimination or reduction with each manager affected by the end product or activity. Ultimately, top management makes the final decisions on which end products and activities will be changed, but in effect all managers (at all levels) affected by any change participate in the process.

This bottom-up approach helps to bring good cost-reduction ideas to the surface. It also helps build a managerial consensus that will pave the way for acceptance of some tough decisions, while limiting resistance to the analytical process itself.

The OVA process consists of five distinct phases, plus a preparatory phase known as Phase 0. The following is a brief description of each phase.

PHASE 0: Preparing for the Program The purpose of Phase 0 is to finalize the program that is designed to meet the specific needs and goals of the department, and to set up the schedule for the project. Also, with the approval of a Steering Committee composed of top management, to select and train the management team that will run the program.

To facilitate analysis, each measurable unit with the department develops its own baseline budget. The baseline budget for each OVA unit is equal to the total of all costs (manpower plus expenses) for that unit for one year. Once this is established, a cost-reduction target (usually 40 percent of the baseline budget) can be set. The 40 percent target is designed to stretch thinking, and to ensure that the activities of each unit is analyzed in a basic and fundamental way. There is *no* expectation that 40 percent will actually be achieved after the different risks are taken into account.

PHASE 1: Developing the Data Base During Phase 1 each OVA unit is broken into components, so that the management team can analyze what it actually accomplishes at what cost, and thus finalize baseline budget. The result is a data base that mirrors each unit and provides the following information about it:

- Description of the missions of the OVA unit. A mission is a statement of purpose that answers the question, *"Why* does this unit exist?"

- Identification of each activity that supports a mission. Activities answer the question, *"How* is a mission accomplished?" (One mission may require the performance of several activities.) Each activity should logically support its mission. In addition, all activities listed must be mutually exclusive, with no overlap.

- Identification of the end products and services that result from activities. End products and services answer the questions, *"What* does a unit produce?" and *"What* are the outputs?" End products are any tangible outputs or services, such as reports, analysis, meetings, advice, instructions. The receivers of each end product are also identified.

- Allocation of costs to each end product. Total end product costs should equal the total cost of resources (the baseline budget) for that unit. Costs of end products are then aggregated for each activity and mission (see Figure 15).

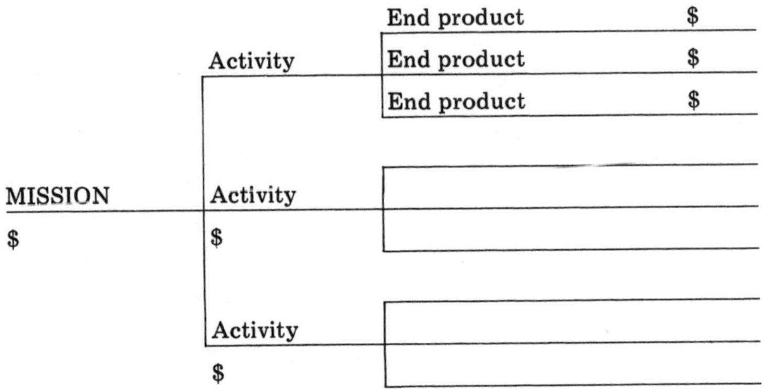

MISSION $	Activity	End product $
		End product $
		End product $
	Activity $	
	Activity $	

Through the courtesy of McKinsey & Company, Inc., New York, N.Y.

FIGURE 15   Structure of Missions, Activities
and End Products

PHASE 2: Generating and Evaluating Ideas The second phase of the program covers the development and evaluation of specific cost-reduction ideas for each OVA unit. All missions, activities, and end products contained in the data base of Phase 1 are analyzed to determine which ones can actually be eliminated, reduced, or streamlined without serious risk to the department and company. The goal is to identify ideas that could reduce the cost of each OVA unit's baseline budget by some 40 percent. Cost-reduction recommendations must represent a broad spectrum of plausible ideas. In general, it is less risky and therefore more desirable to propose many small cuts rather than a few large ones. Members of the selected management team assess the relative risks and benefits of each idea (see Figure 16).

In the end, each member reconciles all comments and evaluations, and puts together a final list of cost-reduction ideas. This list is then submitted to the MIS manager for

GUIDELINES FOR RISK ASSESSMENT

Category of adverse consequences	Elements to consider	Risk Level		
		Low	*Medium*	*High*
Disruption of internal operations and control	— Effects on department or group — Effects on company — Information for decision making			
Reduced employee morale	— Physical environment — Productivity — Grievances — Esprit — Turnover			
Direct adverse effect on financial results	— Company revenue level and growth — Investment required — Expenses			
Inadequate user/ customer service	— Image of MIS department — Existing/ potential users/ customers			

Disruption of vendor relations or timely supply of goods and services	— Stability/ reliability of source of supply — Purchasing cost-effective-ness — Impor-tance of vendor			

Through the courtesy of McKinsey & Company, Inc., New York, N.Y.

FIGURE 16

consideration. The manager reviews all ideas, and may decide to add some of his own. He cannot, however, delete an idea. Once an idea is in the system, it stays there until the Steering Committee makes the final decision. The decisions of the Steering Committee are based on its assessment of the risks involved in the idea.

PHASE 4: Planning Implementation of Approved Ideas
The implementation plan is developed during this phase. The Steering Committee sends all *approved* cost-reduction ideas back to the appropriate unit teams for implementation planning. Each implementation plan must include the following details:

- A full description of the approved idea.
- The specific steps required to implement it.
- All individuals responsible for the implementation.
- A specific timetable for completion of each step of the implementation process.

- The estimated reduction in the unit's budget stemming from each idea implemented.

All implementation plans are then submitted to the DP/MIS manager for approval.

PHASE 5: Implementing the Plans During this phase, actual implementation of approved ideas takes place. Unit teams are responsible for implementing ideas and submitting follow-up progress reports for a certain period to the DP/MIS manager and the Steering Committee.

Parallel Programs In addition to the five phases, two parallel programs play a key role in the OVA process to help ensure its success and lessen threats to personnel security.

The first is man power redeployment that is designed to ease dislocations and minimize terminations, when necessary. This program calls for developing strategies for redeploying and retraining employees whose jobs are eliminated by the OVA process. And for providing support services (job counseling, resume preparation, and so on) for personnel who must be terminated.

The second parallel program deals with communications. A Communications Coordinator is selected and assigned several tasks, such as the following:

- Assist senior management in making visible to the organization its commitment to the program's success.
- Help to communicate program objectives, including the steps being taken to minimize the impact on staff.
- Help to rally support for the program from all levels of management and rank and file.
- Gather feedback from employees (ideas, questions, complaints, and so on) on a regular basis.

125

6.9 COGNITIVE STYLE POSITIONING

A less well-known nonetheless effective strategy for giving job satisfaction to DPers and thus minimizing possible security threats is the "Cognitive Style Positioning." The system, based on research and experiments, shows that people and, more specifically, DP staff approach assignments/projects, situations, problems, and solving of problems differently.

It was found that people may belong to one of the following four defined cognitive styles:

1. The analyzer, who approaches assignments and solving of problems by carefully examining and analyzing all the facts.
2. The evaluator, who approaches assignments and solving of problems in an objective, precise manner.
3. The conceptualizer, who approaches assignments and solving of problems creatively, after seeing the "whole picture" of the situation.
4. The energizer, who can understand the viewpoint of both the DP professionals and the users, and so his approach to assignments and solving of problems relies on good communications.

According to this concept, if the DP employees' cognitive styles are determined, it is up to the MIS manager to "position" or organize each project, each assignment, so that it includes at least one representative of each cognitive style. Because different cognitive-style people work well together as a team, the chances are better that the project —whether it's developing a new system, modifying an old system, or implementing office automation—will be well done and completed on time. And perhaps what is most important from the standpoint of personnel security: cognitive style positioning makes for job satisfaction—the most potent antidote for computer crime.

7

Contingency and Disaster Recovery Planning

SEVEN
Contingency and Disaster Recovery Planning

To insure that DP operations—the lifeblood of business as well as government organizations—resume expeditiously should a disaster occur, a well thought out contingency plan and a comprehensive disaster recovery plan must be in place for the protection and prompt recovery of the organization's critical data and information resources and EDP functions.

A realistic contingency plan that takes into account the human factor will not only minimize the impact of an emergency, regardless of its degree of severity, but also act as a deterrence and detection against computer crime. This is accomplished by the plan defining vulnerable areas and sensitive positions, and making it known that in case of sabotage those areas and positions will be the first to be investigated.

A rigorous, published, tested, and continuously evaluated disaster recovery plan will not only keep an organization going in case of a computer calamity, but provide the fastest and least expensive way to recover by having every person act effectively, whether the disaster is caused by external powers or by an internal computer criminal.

The types of possible catastrophic events at a DP facility can range from *natural disaster* such as fire, flood, tornado, hurricane, or earthquake, to *technical disaster* such as critical hardware breakdown or software malfunction, to *man-made disaster* such as destruction (bombing, arson, and the like), or software or hardware sabotage by a disgruntled employee. Since any one of these disasters can result in serious interruption of business, specific concerns must be addressed to lessen the possible extended loss of the processing of crucial systems.

A study by the University of Minnesota Graduate School of Business Administration concludes that a medium-size bank or a distributing company would go out of business in about *three days* if it could not use its DP facility. While a large bank or a manufacturing company would go out of business in about *four days* if it lost its computer center. According to the study, "most U.S. companies would survive only from one week to one month at most in the event of a major computer disaster."

This dire prediction is supported by a recent study conducted by the National Fire Protection Association. Based on statistics, the study states that an estimated 70 percent of firms will go out of business if a disaster occurs and fire destroys the hardware and software in their computer room. Clearly, the loss of an organization's critical data and information resources as well as the interruption of data processing can be devastating.

Case in point: a Mississippi insurance agency found its DP facility mud-caked and waterlogged last year after a bad flood. Because only a portion of their backup software tapes were off-site (typical of most companies), it took two months for the agency to restore less than half of their data bases. A year later, significant information gaps are still being found in their systems. The dollar cost of restoration was incalculable. The lost man-hours, the cost of consultants, overtime, service bureaus, and alternative work sites brought the company to near bankruptcy.

Yet, because top management tends to ignore the possibility of disasters, according to the latest authoritative estimates some 21 percent of large corporations and some 50 percent of companies with under $100 million in revenues do not have a contingency plan *or* a disaster recovery plan. And if they have a disaster recovery plan, it is often untested and consequently questionable if it works. Many plans look great on paper, but if a disaster occurs would the plans be functional? To put it another way, how could even the best contingency and disaster recovery plans work if their carefully prepared procedures are not tested on trial runs?

Curiously, DP operations, whose very existence may depend on properly executed preventative and recovery procedures in case of a catastrophe, are often the ones that defer testing disaster recovery plans. And the most common excuse for such omission is that DP operations are already behind in their schedule. That they don't have the time or the people to test the plan, let alone test it on a regular basis such as three or four times a year.

All of these reasons may be true, but if management mandates that the computer operations manager's responsibilities include periodic testing of the disaster recovery procedures, it automatically becomes an inherent part of the DP operations schedule.

At this juncture perhaps a clarification of the difference between contingency plan and disaster recovery plan is in order.

7.1 A CONTINGENCY PLAN

A contingency plan—based on risk analysis—identifies the critical information systems and applications that are vital for the company to stay in business. It also determines how often (daily, weekly, or biweekly) those identified systems and applications such as accounts receivable, accounts payable, order entry/inventory control, payroll, and so on, have to run on the computer. Specifically, which software programs are esssential for running the business, and at what intervals are they to be processed. This, in addition to identifying vulnerable areas and sensitive positions.

Further, the contingency plan addresses the concern that if a natural, technical, or man-made disaster, including bomb threat, should occur interrupting computer data processing, what degree of adverse effect would it have on the business? If a disaster struck the DP facility, which systems and applications would have the highest priorities to be run on the backup, off-site, leased or owned computer? Simply put, a contingency plan identifies the company's information resource systems; ascertains the impact of interruption or loss of data processing on the organization's business should a disaster occur; and defines the off-site operations sequence of critical systems on a computer that hopefully has been tested to ensure that the software runs on it as it is supposed to.

Finally, the contingency plan includes a reminder that the company—if it is a publicly held corporation—is required to notify the Securities and Exchange Commission in case it is hit by a disaster.

7.2 A DISASTER RECOVERY PLAN

A disaster recovery plan, on the other hand, is a precise set of written procedures that instructs DP employees exactly what to do—within their own sphere of responsibility—if a natural, technical, or man-made disaster or *the threat* of a disaster occurs at the facility.

7.3 SIDE EFFECTS

If a disaster strikes the computer center, there may be other effects worse than the cost of recovery. The organization—whether it is a manufacturer, insurance, government agency, bank, or whatever—may be exposed to severe penalties because of failure to meet statutory, regulatory, and contractual legal obligations. That is, *if* it can be proven that the organization failed to exercise *due care* by not implementing appropriate contingency plans and disaster recovery arrangements.

In fact, a Federal Government directive, OMBA–123, mandates that any government agency or any company (working under a contract for the government) that uses computer(s) must have a written contingency plan to identify and protect their EDP resources. Furthermore, the Comptroller of the Currency has recently come out with a directive that requires all national banks to have top management approved contingency and disaster recovery plans.

7.4 SOLUTIONS

To avoid any such possible problems, it behooves any company—large or small—that relies on computer system(s) for running and controlling its business to have a written contingency plan *and* a disaster recovery plan that includes detailed procedures. Now, relatively minor disasters, such as hardware or software failures, do happen even at the best managed DP facilities. But they are usually taken care of by the systems programmer or the computer operations supervisor. A single total disaster, however, can be of such magnitude that its possible recovery must be well organized and involve every one of the DP staff, if the organization wants to survive.

Since efficiently carried out disaster recovery procedures can mean the difference between a minimal loss that is slightly more than inconvenience, and a loss that can put the company out of business or at the least push it into a bad financial position, it is imperative to approach DP employees' participation in such crucial undertaking with the human factor in mind. To be specific, convey clearly to personnel the importance of the disaster recovery training sessions; of following the proper procedures in case of a catastrophic event; and of the possible consequences to the company *and* to the DP staff if a disaster "goes down."

After all, you can't expect people to absorb precise instructions and take on responsibilities in a calamity if they don't know what a disaster recovery plan is; if they don't regularly practice the procedures; if they don't know the significance of their actions.

The following steps are recommended as a guide for the DP manager or whoever is responsible for implementing the disaster recovery procedures.

1. In each DP area, such as the computer room, tape library, data control, and I/O, form a *Recovery Team* and assign responsibilities. Give training sessions and periodic testing to each team so that they will know what to do in case of a disaster. Don't overlook, however, giving *recognition* to the teams that do well. Approval boosts team spirit.

2. Publish and distribute the names and extension numbers of the recovery teams, as well as the disaster recovery procedures among all the DP staff.

3. Test the plan three or four times a year by giving a full scale "dry run." This might take some time, effort, and money. But, it can be pointed out to budget-conscious top management, that in case of a disaster, the organization has much to gain from each person knowing what to do.

Case in point: because of a faulty electrical outlet, fire started in one of the supply rooms of a Chicago-based distributing company after office hours. Though the firemen responded promptly to the automatic alarm, the fire spread into the corridor leading to the computer room before it was doused by hundreds of gallons of water.

In the computer room, the swing-shift computer operator at the first sound of the fire alarm reacted quickly. He hit the emergency computer shutdown switch and attended to other necessary preventative measures. He knew just exactly what to do—thus averting possible fire and electrical damage to the equipment and subsequent loss of the company's data—because the firm had a published, tested, and practiced disaster recovery procedures.

Next morning, the computer manufacturer's service engineer (finding nothing wrong with the machine) started up the operations. Thus, computer operations had only a few hours backlog of batch processing, and the loss to the company was minimal.

4. Ask the EDP auditor to test the plan on an unannounced basis. That is, request the auditor to verify if the recovery plan is adequate from *his viewpoint* by simulating a disaster in some critical system and application.

5. Make arrangements with the hardware vendors to expedite repair and/or replacement of damaged or destroyed hardware in case of fire or other disaster at the DP facility.

6. Have an off-site tape storage system, a backup microfiche system, up-to-date lists of hardware and software, accounting records, configuration records, and test data required to rebuild and verify the hardware that may be destroyed partially or completely in a disaster, and re-establish and verify the software environment and location of each item.

Because of the recent many natural disasters that have inflicted heavy damages on private and commercial properties (including DP facilities), such as Hurricane Alicia in August 1983, and floods such as in northern New Jersey in March 1984, there is a burgeoning new industry across the country: off-site storages for the protection of computer media (see Chapter 8, 8.3.2 for definition of media).

These commercial off-site storage companies provide, in addition to safeguarding critical computer media, a courier-service to and from their customers' computer centers for picking up and delivering needed backup data.

7. Rent or lease from one of the many companies in the growing disaster recovery industry either a *"hot site,"* a fully operational computer service facility which is *compatible* with your hardware and software, and provides se-

curity, fire protection, and telecommunications capabilities; or a *"cold site,"* an empty shell which offers space for your mainframe(s) and peripheral equipment, plus electric power, air conditioning, security, and fire protection. The following is a sample listing of available commercial hot sites and cold sites.

FULLY OPERATIONAL COMPUTER SERVICE FACILITIES

Arbat Systems
Arbat Plaza
Hoboken, NJ 07030

Cadre
P.O. Box 687
Avon, CT 06001

Combac Management Corporation
1110 Finch Avenue
Toronto, Ontario M3J2T2

Comdisco Disaster Recovery
6400 Shafer Court
Rosemont, IL 60018

Computer Alternatives
200 North Michigan Avenue
Chicago, IL 60601

Computer Research Co. (Failsafe)
P.O. Box 1138
Doylestown, PA 18901

Disaster Control
555 Goffle Road
Ridgewood, NJ 07450

Hawthorne Computer Service
1234 Market Street
Philadelphia, PA 19181

Litton Mellonics
6701 Variel Avenue
Canoga Park, CA 91303

Neshaminy Valley Information Processing
4850 Street Road
Trevose, PA 19049

Remote Computing Corp.
1076 East Meadow Circle
Palo Alto, CA 94303

Software Research Co.
140 Gold Street
Needham, MA 02194

EMPTY SHELL SITES

Data Shield
P.O. Box 242
Greendale, WI 53129

Data Site
P.O. Box 907
Greenville, RI 02828

Data Processing Security
200 East Loop 820
Fort Worth, TX 76112

Eloigne Corp.
P.O. Box 26312
Minneapolis, MN 55426

Emergency Computer Center
10012 Darnell St.
Lenexa, KS 66215

Martin Marietta Data Systems
P.O. Box 13990
Orlando, FL 32859

National Processing Co.
1231 Durrent Lane
Louisville, KY 40285

Recovery Centers of America
P.O. Box 120122
Nashville, TN 37212

Western-Southern Life Insurance
P.O. Box 1119
Cincinnati, OH 45201

Wright Line/Iron Mountain
160 Gold Star Blvd.
Worcester, MA 01606

8. Ensure that backup copies of the software—*not more than one update behind the current version*—are in the tape library *and* the off-site storage.

9. Keep an up-to-date record of the names, addresses, and phone numbers of the DP facility's systems programmers, computer operator supervisor, and computer operators, and the computer manufacturer's engineers.

10. If using commercial software (who doesn't), keep lists of names, addresses, and phone numbers of vendors' troubleshooters for assistance in case the need arises.

11. Ensure publishing, distributing, *and* periodic updating of the disaster recovery procedures.

12. Ensure, through training sessions, that each DP employee knows:

- *Whom to contact* in certain events
- *What to do* in certain circumstances
- *Who has what responsibility* in case of a disaster
- *Where the backup, or alternative site, or reciprocal arrangement facility is located*
- *Under what circumstances* is the backup or alternative site or other facility to be used

- *Who the contact person(s)* is at the backup, alternative, or reciprocal site.

The bottom line of any contingency and disaster recovery plans should be:

- Do they work satisfactorily in a full-scale disaster, so that the disaster's impact on the firm's business operations is minimal?
- Are they effective in deterring or at least detecting possible computer crime?

8

EDP
Insurance

EIGHT
EDP Insurance

The final component in the deterrence, detection, and prevention of computer crime as it relates to the human factor is *insurance*. Fact of the matter is that, according to some experts, in certain environments such as distributed data processing, for example, where all transactions are done by a legion of multiuser desktop computers, insurance is the only effective crime prevention.

Yet, EDP insurance is a relative newcomer in the insurance field. It was in 1961 that St. Paul Fire and Marine Insurance Company pioneered with an EDP insurance policy that covered large corporations' mainframes. However, with the ubiquitous desktop computers in Fortune 1000 type of organizations, more and more insurance companies are offering EDP insurance policies to cover mainframes as well as mini and/or microcomputers, whether the latter types are used as stand-alones, mainframe-connected, or nodes in a distributed data processing or networking systems.

Now physical, hardware, software, and personnel security measures and controls planned and developed from the human factor viewpoint, and enforced by management will not only prevent or at least minimize errors and the possibility of theft, fraud, and disclosures of information, but will also *lower the premiums on EDP insurance.* Given that most insurance companies *won't insure* companies that do not have effective DP security measures and controls, management does not have much choice but to protect the organization's DP resources.

8.1 EDP INSURANCE VERSUS GENERAL INSURANCE

The argument for separate EDP insurance policy is that standard insurance is not adequate to cover the many and specific risks and potential losses associated with DP operations. In an EDP insurance, contrary to standard insurance, the property value can be fully covered.

Moreover, management has a choice whether to choose the "actual cash value" (purchase price minus depreciation), or "replacement cost" (cost of retail purchase price) type of EDP insurance. Most EDP insurance policies offer both options—with premiums to match.

Final points in the pro-EDP insurance argument are that this specialized insurance usually covers all property (hardware, software, and supplies) in the DP facility *plus* business interruptions. That is, business expenses and losses that incur when some kind of disaster strikes the DP operations. And that EDP insurance—admittedly high—still costs less than buying separate general insurance for each coverage.

8.2 VULNERABLE AREAS AND RISKS

According to a published study, the most often occurring single disaster in DP facilities is *fire,* followed closely by theft and water damage (flood, storm, hurricane). Two major dangers to DP operations, however, were not included. These threats are: electric blackouts and power surges/sags. Either of these events can cause significant damage to the computer systems and the company's business operations *unless* the DP management is smart enough to implement a UPS (uninterruptible power supply), as discussed in Chapter 4.*

It is the DP manager's responsibility, with some assistance from the EDP auditor(s) and the computer security officer, to inform and make top management cognizant of the risks and threats in the DP facility (and throughout the company IF personal computers are used in various offices), and to get support and money for proper preventative measures.

However, it is a management decision as to the amount of an "acceptable loss." That is, how much data processing loss, in case of a disaster or large theft or embezzlement, can the organization take and still stay in business. Furthermore, it is also up to the management to decide which risks—that have been identified, evaluated, and presented in the risk analysis (see Chapter 2)—are to be insured. A lot rides on such decisions, and management is right to take a cautious approach. However, if a loss incurs, and if management has "in force" the appropriate EDP insurance policy, it is the insurance company and *not* the firm that pays for the loss. In other words, all the time and effort that management puts into decision-making about EDP insurance can mean substantial loss or saving for the organization.

---

*There is EDP insurance available for damages caused by electric blackouts and power surges/sags, as well as complete mechanical breakdown. To cover these threats, however, would mean paying higher premiums *and* having higher deductibles.

8.3 AREAS COVERED BY EDP INSURANCE

Areas *usually* covered in an EDP insurance consist of:

- DP equipment and peripheral devices
- Computer media
- Continued DP operations
- Business interruptions

8.3.1 DP Equipment and Peripheral Devices

The EDP equipment and peripheral devices in most basic types of EDP policies are insured against "all risks" such as fire, explosion, smoke, soot, water damage, and collapse of the building. Simply put, "all risks" EDP insurance covers physical destruction or damage of DP and peripheral equipment.

There are, however, usually exclusions such as earthquakes, floods, and war, and definitely theft and fraud by dishonest employees. Some of these exclusions can be insured against, but the premiums and the deductibles are quite high. In fact, in certain parts of the country there is no insurance against earthquakes; while in other areas no insurance is available against floods—additional risk for DP facilities.

8.3.2 Computer media

Computer media include "all forms of converted data such as facts, concepts, or instructions used in the insured data processing operations," which are stored on magnetic tapes, disks, cards or paper tapes (if such antediluvian methods are still around).

The media in most basic types of EDP policies are also insured against "all risks" such as fire, explosion, smoke,

148

soot, water damage, and collapse of building. The exclusions are identical to that mentioned in 8.3.1.

Thus, under media, costs of replacing tapes, disks, and so on, as well as costs of reconstructing data (destroyed in a disaster) from backup systems stored off-site, and other associated costs are usually covered.

8.3.3 Continuted DP Operations

An EDP insurance policy usually covers costs to ensure that DP operations interrupted (destroyed or damaged) by some type of disaster can continue at another facility. This could be at a "hot site," "cold site," or a facility under reciprocal agreement with another computer center using identical or at least similar hardware and operating system.

8.3.4 Business Interruptions

An EDP insurance policy usually covers business interruption expenses that incur when a disaster strikes the DP facility.

8.4 WHITE-COLLAR COMPUTER CRIME INSURANCE

Because of the increase in computer crimes—especially in banks, financial institutions, and government agencies—there is another, though scarce EDP insurance available.

This specialized EDP insurance is against computer theft, fraud, and abuse. As of now, however, only a handful of insurance companies offer such coverage. The fact is that, as stated before, most EDP insurance policies pointedly exclude theft, fraud, and abuse by dishonest staff or consultants.

Lloyd's of London is one of the very few insurance companies that underwrites computer fraud and theft. It has available a specialized EDP insurance against "white-collar" computer crimes in financial institutions. Lloyd's calls it: the "Electronic and Computer Crimes Policies."

8.5 INDIVIDUAL BONDING

Individual fidelity bonding of DP employees who are in money or information-sensitive positions is available from companies who offer EDP insurance policies. Bonding is recommended by security analysts not only because in case the employee commits fraud or embezzlement or theft, the employer is insured against it, but also because it deters computer crime. It does so because the insurance company thoroughly checks the background of each applicant *before* issuing an individual fidelity bonding. Secondly, because the bonded employees are made aware of their responsibility and moral obligation to be honest. And thirdly, they are informed of the dire consequences should any of them commit an illegal act.

Currently, many insurance companies will not issue fidelity bonding on an individual, but only on a group, claiming the risks on individual bonding are too high.

Glossary

ALGORITHM—a definitive set of computational procedures that resolves a problem or performs a mathematical transformation within a finite number of structured steps.

ATM—automatic teller machine.

AUDIT TRAIL—a sequential record of transactions that are input, processed, and output within applications. Audit trails serve EDP auditors to review and examine the accuracy and completeness of the input of source documents; the integrity of the data being processed; and the reliability of the output/report.

BATCH TOTALS—an effective method to ensure that the counted and totaled number and value of similar data items in an input batch are the same *before* and *after* processing. Batch totals enable the system to compare and verify the computer totals against the manually prepared batch totals.

CRYPTOGRAPHY—is the only known current practical means of securing data and information that are transmitted over communications lines such as cable, microwave, fibre-optics, or satellite. A cryptography or encryption system can prevent unauthorized access to sensitive data in transit by enciphering and deciphering data and/or voice.

COLD SITE—a leased empty building or "shell" that offers space for the leaseholder's hardware (mainframe and peripheral equipment), plus electric power and air conditioning.

DATABASE—a collection of interrelated data stored together, using a common and controlled approach.

DATABASE MANAGEMENT SYSTEM (DBMS)—a software package, consisting of a collection of specially designed programs that operate a database or databases.

DES (Data Encryption Standard)—an encryption standard established by the National Bureau of Standards in 1977 and adopted by the American National Standards Institution in 1980 for commercial use. DES consists of a strong algorithm, a 64 bit "private" key, and an S-box —the hardware that implements it. DES or other encryption algorithm is essential for securing telecommunications.

EFT System—electronic funds transfer system. EFT's best known applications are: the Automated Teller Machine (ATM), the Automated Clearing Houses, and the Point-of-Sale (POS).

EDP—electronic data processing.

EDPA (Electronic Data Processing Auditor)—an auditor who, in addition to financial auditing, checks and verifies computer systems software controls, identifies possible errors and vulnerable areas insofar as computer security is concerned, and reports his findings to management. An EDPA performs his functions by studying audit trails, systems documentation, and by using one of the many commercial audit software packages. These specially designed audit programs have become the primary tools for EDPAs in auditing sophisticated computer systems.

EXPORT ADMINISTRATION ACT OF 1979—restricts the sales of national security type of equipment such as microchips, computer hardware and software, and other high technology devices to the USSR and the Soviet bloc countries.

FCPA (Foreign Corrupt Practices Act of 1977)—an amendment to the Securities and Exchange Act of 1934. The Accounting Standards section of the Act mandates that any company subject to the Securities Exchange Act of 1934 shall "(A) make and keep books, records, and accounts, which, in reasonable detail, accurately and fairly reflect the transactions and dispositions of the assets of the company; and (B) devise and maintain a system of internal accounting controls sufficient to provide reasonable assurance that transactions are executed in accordance with management's general or specific authorization."

HASH TOTALS—a useful method to ensure that no items are lost or changed invalidly before or during processing by checking randomly selected fields for meaningless totals such as the total of statements serial numbers, and so on. Hash totals ensure that all data items in a particular batch have been processed, and that the production program has not been tampered with.

HOT SITE—a fully operational leased computer service facility that is compatible with the leaseholder's hardware and software. It provides security, fire protection, and telecommunications capabilities.

INTRUDER DETECTION SYSTEM (IDS)—a software package that alerts the organization's security officer to a person trying to penetrate the system, and identifies the terminal from which the invalid password is being entered.

MAC (Message Authentication Code)—is a technique whereby cryptographic check digits are appended to the message pertaining to the transaction type, transaction account number, destination, and point of origin in computer security. Specifically, by using MAC, messages without the additional check digits are rejected by the computer system, and valid transactions cannot be modified without detection.

MODEM (modulator-demodulator)—a device that enables computers and terminals to communicate with other computers and terminals over telephone lines.

OMBA-123—a Federal Government directive mandating that any government agency or any company working under contract for the government and using computer(s), must have a written contingency plan to identify and protect their EDP resources.

PASSWORD—a set of unique numbers or characters given to a user that allows him to access—according to his level of authorization—files and records for data or information. Users with the highest level of authorization are assigned passwords that allows them to add, change, or update files and programs; while users with low levels of authorization may only read files and programs. And even then, only nonsensive or nonconfidential files and programs may be accessed by the latter group.

PKE (Public Key Encryption)—an encryption algorithm that uses the "public" key approach. Actually, in PKE —in addition to an algorithm—different keys are used at the transmitting and receiving stations. Security of the communications is enforced by protocols.

PRIVACY ACT OF 1974—deals with the right of individuals to control or influence the type and amount of information that may be collected and stored about them, as well as to whom that information may be disclosed.

PROTOCOLS—a set of conventions governing the format and timing of messages between two communicating processes.

RACF (Resource Access Control Facility)—a commercial software package—developed and marketed by IBM—for protecting and monitoring computer systems.

TIMESHARING—a computing method by which several users share the computer's input, processing, and output facilities. Although the computer actually services each user in sequence, the high speed of the processor makes it appear that the users are all handled simultaneously.

UPS (Uninterruptible Power Supply) SYSTEM—provides protection for the DP facility against blackouts, brownouts, power surges/sags, and electrical noises. The latest models of UPS systems use power transistors, making them—contrary to the old, large, and noisy models—small, quiet, and highly efficient.

Bibliography

BATT, ROBERT. "Exec Sees Need for DDP Organizational Changes." *Computerworld* (June 27, 1983): 18.

BEELER, JEFFRY. "Six-Step Method Urged to Tighten Security." *Computerworld* (September 24, 1979): 10.

BEQUAI, AUGUST. "Computer Crime." Lexington, MA: D.C. Heath and Company, 1978.

BEQUAI, AUGUST. "How to Prevent Computer Crime." New York: John Wiley & Sons, 1983.

BRESLIN, JUDSON. "Distributed Processing Systems." New York: AMACOM, 1979.

DAVIS, R.M. "The Data Encryption Standard in Perspective." *IEEE Communications Society Magazine* 16: 6 (1978): 8.

DEMILLO, R. and MERRITT, M. "Protocols for Data Security." *Computer* (February 1983): 39–50.

DIFFIE, W. and HELLMAN, M.E. "New Directions in Cryptography." *IEEE Transactions on Information Theory* 22: 6 (1976): 644.

EASON, T.S. and FITZGERALD, J. "Fundamentals of Data Communications." New York: John Wiley & Sons, 1978.

EDP AUDITORS ASSOCIATION, INC. "Distributed Embezzlement." *The EDP Auditor* (Winter 1980).

FARMER, DALE F. "Confessions of an EDP Auditor." *Datamation* (July 1983): 193–198.

FERRELL, JANE. "How to Keep Computer Data Safe." *San Francisco Examiner* (December 18, 1983): 1, 11–13.

FINE, LEONARD H. "Computer Security." London: Heinemann, 1983.

GRANT, BERNARD J. JR. "Coping With Computer-Related Crime —A Systems Manager's Role." *Proceedings of the First Annual IACSS Conference and Exhibition.* Dix Hills, L.I., NY: International Association for Computer Systems Security, Inc. (1979).

GUYNES, STEVE. "Management, Telecommunications and Computer Security." *Journal of System* 30 (December 1979).

HARRISON, BEN, ed. "Plan for the Worst." *Infosystems* (June 1982): 52–62.

HELLMAN, MARTIN E. "ComSoc Spotlight." *IEEE Communications Society Magazine* 16: 6 (1978): 3.

INOSE, H. "An Introduction to Digital Integrated Communications Systems." Exter, England: A. Wheaton & Co., Ltd., 1979.

KAK, S.C. "Data Security in Computer Networks." *Computer* (February 1983): 8–10.

KENT, S.T. "Encryption-Based Protection for Interactive User/ Computer Communication." *Proceedings, Fifth Data Communications Symposium.* New York: IEEE, 1977.

KIRCHNER, JAKE. "Systems Security Called a Management Issue." *Computerworld* (December 15, 1980): 20.

KRAUSS, LEONARD I, and MACGAHAN, AILEEN. "Computer Fraud and Countermeasures." Englewood Cliffs, NJ: Prentice-Hall, Inc., 1979.

KUO, F.F., ed. "Computer Communications Networks." Englewood Cliffs, NJ: Prentice-Hall, Inc., 1979.

MEYER, CARL H., and MATYAS, STEPHEN M. "Cryptography: A New Dimension in Computer Data Security." New York: John Wiley & Sons, 1982.

MORRIS, R. "The Data Encryption Standard—Retrospective and Prospects." *IEEE Communications Society Magazine* 16: 6 (1978): 12.

POTTRACK, DAVID S. "How to Keep *Distributed* DP Pros Happy." *Focus* (July 1981).

U.S. DEPARTMENT OF JUSTICE. Bureau of Justice Statistics. "Computer Crime Legislative Resource Manual." Washington, D.C. (1980).

U.S. DEPARTMENT OF JUSTICE. Bureau of Justice Statistics. "Computer Crime Expert Witness Manual." Washington, D.C. (1980).

VAN DUYN, J. "Personal Security Policy Critical." *Computerworld* (November 28, 1983): 9–10.

Index

ATM (automatic teller
   machine), 24, 25-27

Blair, Janet, 81
Bruchhausen, Werner J., 11-12

California Penal Code, 13
cipher systems, 52-55
code systems, 51
computer
   crime laws, 14
   and management security
     philosophy, 19-21
   service facilities, 139-141
Counterfeit Access Device and
  Computer Fraud and Abuse
  Act of 1984, 15
crime methods
   data manipulation, 81-82
   piggybacking, 89-90
   rounding down method,
    85-86
   security breach, 91-92
   time bomb method, 83-85

Trojan Horse method,
   82-83
unauthorized accessing,
   90-91

Davis, Justin, 83-85

EDP auditor (EDPA), 62-63,
  81-82, 83, 138
EDP insurance, 145-146
  areas of, 148-149
  and bonding, 150
  versus general insurance, 146
  vulnerable areas and risks,
   146-147
  and white-collar crime,
   149-150
EFT (electronic funds transfer),
  24
encryption systems, 51-55
Equity Funding Life Insurance
  Company (EFLIC), 6-9
Export Administration Act of
  1979, 11

Fields, Ross Eugene, 97,
100–101
Foreign Corrupt Practices Act
of 1977, 5–6

Goldblum, Stanley, 6, 7–9
Gouzene, Gilles, 12–13

Hay System, *see* personnel
security

Lewis, Lloyd Benjamin,
100–102

personnel security
background investigation,
96–99
and budget control,
118–122, 124–125
career-pathing, 99–102
cognitive style positioning,
126–127
and discontent, 102
Hay System, 104–109, 117
and orientation, 102–103
and rotational duties,
117–118
and separation of duties,
103–104
PIN (personal identification
number), 25
planning
contingency, 134–135
disaster recovery, 131–132,
135
and disaster side effects, 135

solutions, 136
Privacy Act of 1974, 10

Rifkin, Stanley Mark, 37–40
risk analysis, 23–28
risk management, 28–29

scavenging, 86–89
Schneider, Jerry Neal, 86–89
Sears Roebuck & Co., 15
Secrist, Ronald, 6–7
security
and air conditioning, 44
approaches, 22–23
access control, 36–41
building and parking lot,
35–36
and data lines, 50–57
and electric power, 47–48
and fire prevention, 42–43
policy and standards manual,
29–32
in storage rooms, 43–44
and terminals, 49–50
see also personnel security
Slear, Eugene B., 96–99
Slyngsted, Stanley, 24–25
smuggling, *see* Bruchhausen,
Werner J.; Gouzene, Gilles
software
applications control, 71–77,
80
and corporate policy, 64–65
protection systems, 65
systems and programming
standards, 66, 68, 70